Ontario's Waterfalls

A Complete Guide

Ontario's Waterfalls
A Complete Guide
for Photographers and Explorers

Copyright 2013 Harold Stiver

ISBN # 978-0-9917760-9-2

Photo Credits

All photographs are the work of the author, Harold Stiver for which he holds the copyright and reserves all rights.

Table of Contents

The Waterfalls

Niagara Region

Balls Falls, Balls Falls (Upper), Beamer Falls, Beamer Falls (Lower), Beamer Side Falls, Decew Falls, Decew Falls(Lower), East 18 Mile, Faucet Falls, Hillside Cascade, Louth Falls, Louth Falls (Upper), Lynn River Falls (Norfolk), Martins Falls, Middle 18 Mile, Niagara Falls, Rockway Falls, Swayze Falls, Terrace Falls, Thirty Road Falls, West 18 Mile

Hamilton Region

Albion Falls, Auchmar Falls (Upper Beckett Falls), Baby Albion Falls,Baby Webster Falls,Beckett Falls (Lower Beckett Falls), Betzner Falls (Lower Weir's Falls), Billy Green Falls (Battlefield Falls), Billy Monkley Cascade, Borer's Falls Lower, Borer's Falls (Rock Chapel Falls), Boundary Falls, Broman Falls, Brown Falls, Buttermilk Falls,

Canterbury Falls (Milne Falls), Cave Falls, Centennial Falls, Chedoke Falls Lower, Chedoke Falls, Clappison Falls, Cliffview Falls Lower, Cliffview Falls, Darnley Cascade (Stutts Falls), Deal Cascade, Denlow Falls, Devil's Punchbowl Lower, Devil's Punchbowl (Horseshoe Falls), Dewitt Falls, Duchess Falls, Dundas Falls, Dyment Falls, East Glover's Falls, East Iroquoia Falls, Erland Falls, Felker's Falls, Ferguson Falls, Fifty Road Cascade, Fruitland Falls Lower, Fruitland Falls Upper, Glendale Falls Lower, Glendale Falls Middle (Glendale Cascade), Glendale Falls Upper (Glendale Falls), Glover's Falls, Grand Cascade, Great Falls (Grindstone Falls, Waterdown Falls, Smokey Hollow Falls), Greensville Falls, Grindstone Cascade, Hannon Cascade, Heritage Falls (Griffin Falls), Heritage Green Falls, Hermitage Cascade (Hermitage Falls), Hidden Grindstone Falls, Hopkins Cascade Lower, Hopkins Cascade Upper, Hunter Falls, James Falls, Jones Road Falls, Lafarge Falls, Lewis Road East Falls, Lewis Road West Falls, Little Canterbury Falls, Little Davis Falls, Little Falls Lower on Wilson, Little Falls on Wilson, Little Rock Chapel Falls (Rock Chapel Road Falls), Lower Mills Falls, Lower Sydenham Falls, McNeilly Falls, Middle Sydenham Falls, Mineral Springs Falls, Mountain Spring Falls, Mountview Falls, Oak Knoll Falls, Old Dundas Road Falls, Optimist Cascade, Patterson East Cascade, Patterson West Cascade, Pond Falls Lower, Pond Falls, Princess Falls Lower (Lang's Falls), Princess Falls Upper, Pritchard Falls, Progrestron Falls, Promontory Falls, Ridge Falls, Sanatorium Cascade Lower (Lower Sanatorium Falls), Sanatorium Falls (Upper Sanatorium Falls, Sanatorium Ravine), Scenic Falls, Shaver Falls Upper (Upper Filman Falls), Shaver Falls (Filman Falls), Sherman Falls (Fairy Falls, Angel Falls), Sisters of Mary Falls (Upper Canterbury Falls), Spring Falls (Upper Grindstone Falls, Arnolds Falls), Springhill Falls, Stephanie Falls, Steven's Falls, Tallman East Falls (Vinemount East Falls), Tallman West Falls (Shed Falls), Tews Falls Lower (Baby Tews Falls, Hopkins Ravine), Tew's Falls (Hopkin's Falls), Thomas Falls, Tiffany Falls, Troy Falls, Upper Mills Falls, Upper Sydenham Falls, Valley Falls, Veever's Falls, Vinemount East Falls (Vinemount Middle Falls), Vinemount West Falls, Wall Falls, Walnut Grove Falls, Washboard Falls (Upper Tiffany Falls), Webster's Falls (Fisher's Falls, Flamborough Falls, Hatt's Falls, Spencer's Falls), Weir's Falls (Upper Weir's Falls), West Iroquoia Falls, West McNeilly Falls, West of Fifty Cascade (West of Fifty Upper Cascade), Westcliffe Falls Lower, Westcliffe Falls, Winona Falls (East of Fifty Falls)

South Central Region   Page 69

Bruce County: Barrows Bay Falls, Colpoys Falls, Cypress Lake Outlet Falls, Sauble Falls

Dufferin County: Canning Falls Lower, Canning Falls Upper, Horning Mills, Scott Falls Lower, Scott Falls Upper

Grey County: Antheas Waterfall, Epping Falls, Eugenia Falls, Fairmount Falls, Hayward Falls, Hoggs Falls, Indian Falls, Inglis Falls, Jones Falls, Keefer Falls, Maxwell Falls, McGowan Falls, Minniehill Falls, Oxenden Falls, Traverston Cascade, Walters Falls, Weaver Creek Falls(Harrison Park Falls)

Halton County: Hilton Falls, Kilbride Falls, Limehouse Rapids, Quarry Cascade Lower, Quarry Cascade Middle, Silver Creek Falls, Snake Falls Lower, Snake Falls Upper, Snow Creek Falls North, Snow Creek Falls West

Huron County: Falls Reserve

Lambton County: Ausable River Falls, Rock Glen (Fuller Falls)

Peel County: Belfountain Falls, Churches Falls, Churches Falls (Upper)

Waterloo County: Devils Creek, Devils Creek (West)

Wellington County: Elora Gorge, Everton Cascade, Fergus Cascade, Irvine Creek Cascade, Little Elora Waterfall, Rockwood Falls

Cottage Country Region

Haliburton County: Brandy Falls, Buttermilk Falls(Haliburton), Castor Oil Chute, Cope Falls, Drag River Falls, Elliott Falls, Furnace Falls, Gooderham Falls, Gut Rapids, High Falls (York at Kennaway), Kennisis Falls, Kinmount Cascade, Long Slide, Minden Whitewater Preserve, Moore Falls, Nunikani Dam Falls, Rackety Falls, Ragged Falls, Ritchie Falls (Lower), Ritchie Falls (Middle), Ritchie Falls (Upper), The Buckslides, Three Brothers Falls, Tim Road Cascades, Tim Road Falls, Witney Rapids

The Kawarthas: Big Eddy, Fenelon Falls, Ragged Rapids, Victoria Falls

Muskoka County: Bala Falls, Bala Falls 2, Baysville Dam, Big Chute (Severn), Big Eddy Rapids, Bracebridge Falls (Lower), Bracebridge Falls (Upper), Bullhead Falls, Clark Falls, Crozier Falls, Curtain Chute, Dee Bank Falls, Distress Chute, Duck Chutes, Fairy Falls, Flat Rapids, Flat Rock Rapids, Go Home Chute, Gravel Falls, Hanna Chute, Hardy Lake Falls, Hatchery Falls, High Falls (Bracebridge), Hogs Trough, Hood Rapids, Island Portage Falls, Kashe River Cascade, Little High Falls, Marsh Falls, Matthiasville Falls, May Chutes, McCutcheons Falls, McDonald River Falls, Minnehaha Falls(Muskoka), Moon Falls, Muskoka Falls, Mye River Cascades, Ox Tongue Rapids, Peterson Falls, Port Sydney Falls, Potts Falls, Pretty Channel Rapids, Rosseau Falls (Lower), Rosseau Falls (Upper), Sandy Gray Rapids, Slater Falls, Stubbs Falls, Tea Falls, Three Rock Chute, Trethewey Falls, Twin Falls Upper, Whites Falls, Wilsons Falls

Simcoe County: Coopers Falls, Lavender Falls, Little Falls, Port Severn Rapids, Wasdell Rapids

Eastern Region

Frontenac County: Bedford Mills Falls, Belleville Rapids, Birch Rapids, Black Rapids, Kings Chute, Kings Falls, Kingston Mills Falls, Ragged Chute, Whitefish Rapids

Hastings County: Big Chute, Callaghan Rapids, Chisholm Mills, Cordova Falls, Egan Chute, Farm Chute, High Falls (Actinolite), High Falls (Papineau Creek), High Falls (York River), Jelly Rapids, McArthur Falls, Middle Chute, Neuman Falls, Price Rapids, Robinson Falls, The Gut, Triplebee Falls

Lanark County: Appleton Rapids, Arklan Rapids, Blakeney Rapids, Carleton Place Cascade, Chaffey Lock Cascade, Grand Falls, Mill Falls, Mill of Kintail Rapids, Old Sly Lockes Cascade, Smiths Falls , Tays Rapids

Leeds and Grenville County: Jones Falls Waste Weir

Lennox and Addington County: Babcock Mill Cascade, Buttermilk Falls (Forest Mills), Crooked Slide, Flinton Falls, Forest Mills, Millhaven Falls, Napanee Falls, Newburgh Falls, Yarker Falls

Northumberland County: Campbellford Rapids (Crowe Bay Rapids), Crowe Bridge Rapids, Healey Falls, Ranney Falls

Ottawa-Carleton County: Cardinal Creek Falls, Chat Falls, Chaudiere Falls, Fitzroy Cascade, Fitzroy Falls, Galetta Falls, Orleans Falls, Rideau Falls, The Hog's Back

Peterborough County: Burleigh Falls, Haultain Cascade, High Falls (Apsley), High Falls (Eels), Marble Rapids, Mississauga Cascade, North River Cascade, Perry's Creek Cascade, South Eels Cascade, Three Bears Rapids, Warsaw Caves Falls

Prescott and Russell County: High Falls (Casselman), Jessups Falls

Renfrew County: Aumonds Rapids, Barron Canyon Rd Falls, Bonnechere Falls, Exam Time Rapids, Fifth Chute, Fourth Chute Lower Fourth Chute Upper, Grants Creek Falls, Hyland Falls, Jacks Chute, Old Killahoe Cascade, Pakenham Falls, Rifle Chute, Second Chute, Slate Falls, Split Rock Rapids, Third Chute, A Mystery Waterfall, Conroy Rapids

Northeast Region ` Page 128

Cochrane County: Kapkigiwan Falls, Keneki Lake Falls, New Post Falls, Sandy Falls (Cochrane), Thunder House Falls, Wawaitan Falls

Manitoulin County: Bridal Veil Falls (Kagawong), High Falls (Manitoulin)

Nipissing County: Allen Rapids, Battery Rapids, Brigham Chute, Carcajou Falls, Cascade Rapids, Cedar Lake Falls, Crooked Chute, Crow River Falls, Crystal Falls (Sturgeon), Devils Cellar Rapids, Devils Chute, Duchesnay Falls (East), Duchesnay Falls (West), Eau Claire Gorge Falls, Galipo River Falls, Gravelle Chute, Grillade Rapids, Gut Rapids, High Chute, High Falls (Barron), High Falls (Little Bonnechere R.) , High Falls (Nipissing R), Laurel Lake Falls, Lion Chute, Long Rapids, Mew Lake Cascade, North Tea Falls, Observatory Falls, Palmer Rapids, Paresseaux Falls, Peddler's Falls Pen-to-Rock Falls, Petit Paresseaux Falls, Red Pine Chute, Sandy Falls, Shirley Lake Falls, Squirrel Rapids, Sturgeon Falls, Talon Chute, White Horse Rapids

Parry Sound County: Big Jameson Rapids, Big Parisien Rapids, Big Pine Rapids, Bingham Chute, Blue Chute, Broadbent Falls, Brooks Falls, Bunny Trail Falls, Burk's Falls, Chapmans Chute, Cody Rapids, Corkery Falls, Cox Chute, Crooked Rapids (French), Davidson Chute ,Devils Chute (French River), Devil Door Rapids, Double Rapids, Dutchman Chutes, Elliott Chute, Fagans Falls, Five Mile Rapids , Freeman Chute, Geisler Chute, Gimball Chute, Hab Rapids, Herring Chutes, Horseshoe Falls, Indian Rapids, Knoefli Falls, Liley Chute, Little Jameson Rapids, Little Parisien Rapids, Little Pine Rapids, Lower Burnt Chute, MacIndoo Falls, Magnetawan Lock, Mahzenazing Cascade, McNab Chute, Mountain Chute (Seguin), Needle Eye Rapids, Old Man River Falls, Pickerel Lake Rd Cascade, Porter Rapids, Poverty Bay Chutes, Ragged Rapids (Manitouwabin), Recollet Falls, Restoule Falls, Ross Rapids, Seller Rapids, Serpent Rapids, South River Cascade, Stirling Falls, Stovepipe Rapids, Thirty Dollar Rapids, Thompson Rapids, Truisler Chute, Upper Burnt Chute, Wasi Cascade, Wasi Falls

Sudbury County: Bear Chutes, Cameron Falls, Cascade Falls, Centre Falls, Chartrand Corners Falls, Conniston Hydro Dam, Duncan Chute, Espanola Falls, Floodwood Chutes, Frank Falls, Gordon Chutes, Helen Falls, High Falls (Spanish), Kenogamissi Falls, Kettle Falls, Larchwood Cascade, Lorne Falls, Lower Goose Falls, Massey Chute, McCharles Lake Cascade, McFadden Falls, McVittie Dam Falls, Meshaw Falls, Nairn Falls, Onaping Falls, Plunge Falls, Sagamok Falls, Secord Road Cascade, Seven Sisters Rapids, Sturgeon Chutes, The Chutes, Timmins Chute, Upper Goose Falls, White Pine Chutes, Whitefish Falls

Algoma Region `   Page 156

Agawa Falls, Airport Road Falls, Aubrey Falls, Baldhead River Falls, Batchawana Falls, Beaver Falls, Bells Falls, Bellevue Creek Falls, Big Carp River Falls, Black Beaver Falls North, Black Beaver Falls South, Bridal Veil Falls (Algoma), Cataract Falls, Chippewa Falls, Chippewa Falls (upper), Coldwater River Falls, Crystal Falls, Dore Falls, Goulais River Falls Granary Creek Falls, Grand Falls, Grindstone Falls, Harmony River Falls, High Falls (Blind River), Kennebec Falls, Lady Evelyn Falls, Little Rapids, McCarthy Chute, McPhail Falls, Michipicoton Harbour Rd Falls, Minnehaha Falls(North), Mississagi Falls, Montreal River Chasm, Otter Creek, Pancake Falls, Pecors Falls, Potholes Falls, Robertson Creek Falls, Root Falls, Sand River Falls Lower, Sand River Falls Upper, Scott Falls, Silver Falls (Lower), Silver Falls (Middle), Speckled Trout Falls, Split Rock Rapids, Steep Hill Falls, Thessalon Falls (Lower), Thessalon Falls (Upper), Thunder Falls, Wawa Falls, Whitefish Falls (Little Missiniabi River)

Lakehead Region   Page 173

Kenora County: Nestor Falls, Oak Falls, Raleigh Falls, Rushing River

Rainy River County: Canyon Falls, Little Falls (Atikokan), Kennebas Falls, Koko Falls, Silver Falls (Atikokan River), Snake Falls, Split Rock Falls

Thunder Bay County: Aguasabon Falls, Alexander Falls, Angler Falls, Cameron Falls (Nipigon), Cascade Falls (Cascade), Cascade Falls (Current River), Chigamiwinigun Falls, Dead Horse Creek Falls, Denison Falls, Dog Falls, High Falls (Kaministiquia River), High Falls of the Pigeon River, Hume Falls, Kakabeka Falls, Kinghorn Falls, Last Falls on Cypress, Lenore Lakes Falls, Long Rapids, MacKenzie Falls, Mazukama Creek Falls, Middle Falls, Middle Falls on Cypress, Mink Creek Falls, Partridge Falls, Pine River Falls, Port Arthur Spillway, Rainbow Falls, Schist Falls, Sevignys Creek Falls, Silver Falls (Kaministiquia River), Split Falls, Spring Falls, Trowbridge Falls, Twin Falls, Umbata Falls, Upper Falls on Cypress

Introduction

Waterfalls are a healing balm to the weary soul. The transitory beauty of falling water, a beautiful setting and the bubbling music of a million drops releases us from the stress and noise of a hectic life.

If you visit waterfalls, you will find yourself in varied company, from seasoned hikers to casual family groups, old and young alike, fall under their spell. Even those otherwise indifferent to wilderness and nature often succumb to their charms.

Ontario is larger than many countries of the world and has been blessed with an incredible variety of beautiful natural areas. These include areas like the Canadian shield and the Niagara escarpment which are great spots for waterfalls in wonderful settings.

This book has been structured under 8 Regions as follows:

Niagara Region: This area which includes Niagara and Haldiman County contains some of the finest waterfalls in Ontario.

Hamilton Region: Comprised of Hamilton-Wentworth Municipality, is has a large number of waterfalls listed primarily because of the work of some dedicated people who have made an active effort to catalogue them.

South-Central Region: Includes the counties of Bruce, Dufferin, Grey, Halton, Huron, Lambton, Peel, Waterloo and Wellington. There are some excellent falls here because of the presence of the Niagara Escarpment.

Cottage Country Region: Includes the counties of Haliburton, Muskoka and the Kawarthas. There are some excellent and diverse waterfalls spread through this region.

Eastern Region: Made up of the counties of Frontenac, Hastings, Lanark, Leeds and Grenville, Lennox and Addington, Northumberland, Ottawa-Carleton, Peterborough, Prescott and Russell, and Renfrew.

Northeast Region: Includes the counties of Cochrane, Manitoulin, Nipissing, Parry Sound and Sudbury.

Algoma Region: Algoma County has some excellent waterfalls including those seen on the Agawa Canyon Train Trip.

Lakehead Region: Includes the Counties of Kenora, Rainy River and Thunder Bay. Some of the largest and finest waterfalls are found in this area.

Safety

Lets start with a simple fact, people have died at waterfalls in Ontario and many more have been hurt. The combination of height and possible slippery conditions can be dangerous. Consider the following:
Wear appropriate footwear
Dress warmly in layers and bring rain gear
Take an adequate water supply and never drink from streams
Travel with a partner when possible
Let someone know where you are going and when you will be back
Check the weather report and keep an eye out for changing conditions
Areas containing waterfalls may be open to hunting, take suitable precautions
You should also be aware that in early morning ice will often form on rocks and trails from waterfall spray even when the temperature is above freezing.
Some waterfalls, such as Aubrey Falls, have dams upstream that periodically release water. If you are caught out on the rocks above or below these falls when this happens, you may be in extreme danger.

How to use this book

The waterfalls in this book are described by two types of citations, a long form is reserved for the more outstanding sites and a shorter form for lesser sites. While it would have been great to give all of the 600 plus sites an extended citation, it was not feasible due to size constraints.

Both formats contain the following information.

Name of the falls and common **alternate names**

The region: We have divided Ontario into 8 regions: Niagara, Hamilton, South Central, Cottage Country, Eastern Ontario, Northeast, Algoma and the Lakehead.

The county: Each site has the county it is in listed.

Nearest town: As an aid to locations, the nearest town or Government park is shown

Type of falls: The structure of the falls is listed.

Many of Ontario's waterfalls have been altered or many have disappeared due to hydro electric projects. A lot of them are still worth visiting. For those sites we know to have these obstructions, note has been made in their citation.

Water source: The river or creek name

Our ratings: Our subjective rating based on things like height, width, lack of obstructions or man made elements, and the total setting. The ratings break down as follows:

One Star For Collectors Only:
If you are not an obsessed fanatic, you may want to pass this one by. This may be because it is seasonal, clogged with unattractive debris, has ugly mad made elements, or offers no good viewing and photo opportunities.

Two Stars Average Interest:
Well worth a visit, this waterfall will offer an interesting viewing and
photo experience. There may be occasions when it has been dry
weather were the flow may be down, but usually you can expect a good
visit.

Three Stars Very Good:
This waterfall has a lot to offer, and worth considerable effort to visit.
Except for a few instances, it offers a natural experience without man
made objects, multiple viewing and photo opportunities, and an overall
memorable experience.

Four stars Awesome!!
Go see these waterfalls!! There are about two dozen waterfalls in
Ontario with this rating and they are worth a considerable effort to see.
Do a little research before you go to be sure you get the best of it, and
make sure you allow yourself plenty of time to visit.

Access: Ranging from easy to difficult, this will give you some idea of
what is involved in reaching the site.

GPS Location: GPS positions are given for all sites. In many cases it is
for nearby parking areas as many GPS devices will not locate off road
positions. These positions can also be entered into mapping programs
such as Google Maps.

Additionally the large citations have the following information.

Description: Information about the waterfall and its surroundings.

Getting there: Written directions to find the site.

Nearby Attractions: Other waterfalls in the immediate area.

Types of waterfalls

There is no accepted naming systems for the different waterfall structure types but the following are commonly noted. Some of them are synonymous.

Block: Refers to a falls the extends across most of the width of the water source, generally wider than it is tall.

Cascade: The water drops in a series of falls, usually irregular in size and often in contact with the bedrock. It can often become clogged with boulders and fallen tree limbs.

Chute: When a river is compressed in a narrow vertical passage, it is referred to as a chute.

Curtain: A waterfall whose height is notably smaller than its crest width.

Horsetail: This type of falls fans out as it drops while staying in contact with the bedrock.

Overfall: This type of falls, usually small, is the result of a hump in the bedrock in an otherwise fairly level course. It causes the water to become turbulent as it rises over it.

Plunge: The water fall is vertical and loses contact with the bedrock.

Punchbowl: Characterized by a narrow width falls terminating in a large plunge pool.

Ribbon: Water falls in a thin strip, significantly taller than it is wide.

Slide Falls: A waterfall which flows down a steeply sloping rock face. It is usually a smooth surface.

Step or tiered: The water drops in a series of distinct falls or steps

Photographing Waterfalls

Waterfalls offer a unique setting to compose interesting images. They also offer interesting problems to be solved, chiefly ones of exposure as well as dealing with the movement of the water. They also are scenes which allow you to work the site, to make images which range from the waterfall as part of to those the key in on only a small portion of the falling water.

These beautiful places have something to offer in all seasons. In spring they are often full and raging, while in summer they may be more gentle but includes scenes of green growth as contrast. Fall can add stunning foliage while winter includes the wonders of ice and snow.

Basic equipment

Many cameras may be suitable and a wide lens can be very useful. I use a 17-40mm zoom for 95% of my photographs. I would highly recommend using a tripod, as the increased stability makes a huge difference in the sharpness of an image. A polarizing filter can also be very valuable in cutting unwanted reflections off both water and foliage.

Dealing with exposure

One of the first problems you will face with waterfall photography is overexposure of certain portions of the image like the water or sky. Part of this problem can be solved in your composition by eliminating the sky as much as possible. It can also be helpful to pick an overcast day in order to minimize the exposure range.

For many years experienced photographers have taken different exposures and blended the results. This process has been automated by the use of software which blends different exposures of the same image in a process known as High Dynamic Range or HDR.

Using HDR(High Dynamic Range)

HDR is a process where multiple images of varying exposure are combined to make one image.

It has a bad name with some people because many HDR images are super-saturated, a kind of digital age version of an Elvis painted on velvet. However, the process is actually about getting a full range of exposure with no burnt out highlights or blocked shadows. This is an ideal processing solution for photographing waterfalls where very high exposure water as well as open sky contrasted against dark shadowed landscape. This is often outside the range of exposure that most cameras can cover in a single image but multiple images of different exposure does the job nicely when combined.

I often use a series of three exposures at levels of -2, 0, +2, and this normally runs the full exposure range encountered. It is important to use a stable tripod.

If you are looking for a natural result, it is important to have a light hand on the controls when processing.

There are a number of software programs you can use to combine these images including newer editions of Photoshop. I use Photomatix which I have found very versatile and easy to use.

Type of flow

Another decision the photographer needs to make is what the movement of the water looks like. You can have the water look blurred, a silky flow, or very detailed, showing individual drops. The former has become favored but you should also look at the detailed result which can give you wonderful images as well.

What results you end up with are based on shutter speed. To get that silky effect, you will need to have a slow shutter speed. The speed varies but usually you will want to get it to at least 1/125 sec and probably even slower.

To reach these slow shutter speeds, you can decrease your ISO to 100 and decrease your focal length to f/22. If this is not sufficient you can make use of Neutral density filters which cut the amount of light reaching the lens. using HDR techniques always results in blurred water.

Tours

The Agawa Canyon Train Tour

The Agawa Canyon Train Tour is one of the finest attractions available in Canada. The Algoma Central Railway runs a day trip from Sault Ste. Marie north for 114 km to Agawa Canyon. It travels through lakes and wilderness, often crossing tall wooden trestles, and in the right season the foliage is something you will always remember.

The excursion runs from the last week in June to the middle of October. I recommend the middle of September to the first week in October for the full effect of the autumn foliage. You should book early for these periods. You can book by telephone by calling 1-800-242-9287 or online at http://www.agawacanyontourtrain.com

The large coach windows are ideal for viewing as the train travels to the canyon. There is an hour and a half stop at the canyon for you to explore. There are four waterfalls at the canyon, Bridal Veil, Black Beaver North and South and Otter Falls. I would recommend visiting them in that order which allows you to visit the best ones first and performs a loop from the train and back. After Otter falls you will pass a set of steps which lead to a bird's eye view of the canyon which you can do if you have the time and energy.

There is a restaurant car on the train and plenty of hotel rooms in Sault Ste. Marie. The train depot is at 129 Bay Street in Sault Ste. Marie.

Niagara Region Tour

The Niagara Region is famous for Niagara Falls but there are a number of other excellent waterfalls to see. There are three stops but five falls to see, as well as two mills.

Falls	Page	Rating
Balls Falls Upper	31	3/4
Balls Falls Lower	30	4/4
Rockway Falls	38	4/4
Martins Falls	37	1/4
Decew Falls	34	3/4

We start the tour at Balls Falls Upper (N 43° 7.688' W 79° 23.053'). Go north on Highway 24 (Victoria St.) off of Highway 401 Niagara. As you are going up the escarpment, turn left on Sixth Ave, and drive a short way to the parking area (Fee). The Upper falls is beside the mill on the other side of the road. To reach Lower Balls Falls, cross the road and take the trail on either side of Twenty Mile Creek and a 15 minute walk will bring you to it. I prefer the views from the east side (the side where the visitor center is located).

Our next stop is Rockway Falls (N 43° 6.672' W 79° 19.224'). Go back to Victoria Ave and turn left on 8th Ave/Pelham Rd.. After 1.4 km. turn left and drive 3.6 km. to Rockway and park at the Community Center. The falls is behind the center, please be careful as there are no rails. After visiting this falls, walk to the bridge by the Community Center and look in the other direction to see Martins Falls which is on private property. It is easy to see from the public road.

Our last stop is Decew Falls (N 43° 6.617' W 79° 15.816'). Continue east on Pelham Rd. for 4.3 km and turn right on First Street Louth, continuing on Decew Road. You will reach the falls and the mill in 1.9 km. There are two other falls downstream (Lower Decew and Faucet Falls) but they are difficult to get to, read the citations for them.

This finishes our Niagara Region Tour.

Hamilton Premier Tour

Hamilton boasts about 150 waterfalls and this tour gets you to some of the best of them.

Falls	Page	Rating
Websters Falls	67	4/4
Tews Falls	63	3/4
Borers Falls	44	3/4
Great Falls	53	3/4
Tiffany Falls	64	3/4
Sherman Falls	61	3/4

We start at Websters Falls (N 43° 16.544' W 79° 58.816') considered by many as the best in the area. You can reach this area by taking Brock Rd. south off of Highway 5. Turn left onto Harvest Rd, and then right onto Short Rd, which will shortly lead you to parking for the conservation area. There is a great deal to explore here.

Our next stop is Tews Falls (N 43° 16.85' W 79° 58.6') Go west on Fallsview Rd/Short Rd and turn right on Harvest Rd. The parking for Tews Falls is about 0.7 km. Tews is Hamilton's highest waterfall.

We will now head for Borers Falls (N 43° 17.592' W 79° 56.192') Go east on Harvest Rd and after 2.3 km continue on Sydenham Rd. and then Rock Chapel Rd. The falls is 1.4 km but there is a parking area at the road bend shortly before you get there. Be careful walking along the roadside.

Our next destination is Great Falls in Waterdown (N 43° 19.8 W 79° 53.233) Continue north on Rock Chapel Road and after 1.3 km turn right on ON-5 which becomes Dundas St. In 5 km turn right on Mill St and after 0.5 km you will see a parking area on the right side. The trail from this spot is another great way to spend some time.

We now head for Tiffany Falls (N 43° 14.436' W 79° 57.594'). Continue east on Mill St. which becomes Waterdown Rd. and after 3 km, turn right onto Ontario 403. After 12.7 km take exit 64 and merge onto Mohawk Rd which becomes Rousseaux St. In 2.6 km turn right on Wilson St and in 1.7 km you will see the parking lot for Tiffany

Falls. The trail leads to the base of the falls. This is one of the best looking falls in winter.

Our last stop is Sherman Falls (N 43° 14.3' W 79° 58.383') Backtrack west on Wilson St. and after 1 km. turn right on Montgomery Dr. In 0.2 km turn right on Old Dundas Rd. Drive 0.2 km and just past the 1st intersection, park by the side of the road and take the trail to the north.

This is the end of our tour.

Chedoke Rail Trail

The Chedoke Rail Trail in Hamilton parallels the Chedoke Expressway/Highway 403 as it climbs the escarpment. It provides a number of good waterfalls to view and a nice walk as well. All of these falls can range from raging to a trickle so you may want to go after a good rainstorm or during the spring melt.

Falls	Page	Rating
Lower Cliffview Falls	48	2/4
Lower Westcliffe Falls	68	2/4
Lower Sanatorium Falls	60	2/4
Princess Falls	59	2/4
Princess Falls Lower	59	2/4

We join the Chedoke Rail Trail at the south end of Beddoe Cr. in Hamilton. As we face the escarpment we head right or west and shortly we will see the double waterfall of Lower Cliffview Falls and Lower Westcliffe Falls (N 43° 14.717' W 79° 54.5')Farter up on both water sources is Upper Cliffview Falls and Upper Westcliffe Falls which can be reached through a strenuous hike.

As we proceed west we will come to Lower Sanatorium Falls (N 43° 14.754' W 79° 54.888') which has had its floor artificially constructed in an interesting manner. There is an Upper Sanatorium Falls but it is best accessed from the top of the escarpment.

As we continue our walk, we come to Princess Falls and a peak over the escarpment reveals Lower Princess Falls (N 43° 14.75' W 79° 55.733'). There is another waterfall called Duchess Falls on the other side of the highway which is a continuation of this system.

While this is the end of our tour, you could proceed farther and search out Scenic Falls as well as East and West Iroquoia Falls

Owen Sound Tour

The town of Owen Sound boasts some excellent waterfalls and we will visit four of them.

Falls	Page	Rating
Inglis Falls	72	3/4
Weaver Creek Falls	75	2/4
Jones Falls	73	3/4
Indian Falls	71	3/4

We start our tour at Inglis Falls (N 44° 31.583' W 80° 56.072'). A few miles south of Owen Sound, take Grey Rd. 18 off of Highway 6. Look for Inglis Falls Rd, on your right. there is a boardwalk across from the falls which provides great views.
Our next stop is Weaver Creek Falls (N 44° 32.556' W 80° 56.280'). Go north on Inglis Falls Rd and after 2 km. turn right on 2nd Ave SE/E. Proceed into Harrison Park and continue to the pool area. The falls is found near the end of the short trail that begins near the pool.

Now we head for Jones Falls (N 44° 33.55' W 80° 59.103') Go back to 2nd Ave E. and then go north for 1.9 km and turn left on 10th St. E/ON-21 which becomes 10th St. W shortly. After 3.8 km. you will be climbing the escarpment. Look for a pull off and trail to the falls.

Our final stop is Indian Falls (N 44° 37.267' W 80° 57.25'). backtrack on 10th St. W/ON-21 for 3.5 km and turn left on 2nd Ave W. This becomes 3rd Ave W and then Grey Road 1. After 5 km, you will see the entrance to Indian Falls Conservation Area. The trail takes about 15 minutes to the falls.

This ends our tour

Bracebridge Tour

The Bracebridge tour involves four stops but you get to see seven falls.

Falls	Page	Rating
Muskoka Falls	98	3/4
Bracebridge Falls Upper	90	3/4
Bracebridge Falls Lower	89	3/4
Wilsons Falls	103	3/4
High Falls	94	3/4
Potts Falls	100	2/4
Little High Falls	96	2/4

Our first stop is Muskoka Falls (N 44° 59.514' W 79° 17.867'). From ON-11 take exit 184 and follow Cedar Lane/ Frederick St Rd then keep left at the fork and follow the signs for Muskoka Falls.

Our next stop is Bracebridge Falls, Upper and Lower (N 45° 2.317' W 79° 18.483'). Head northeast on ON-118/Reg. Rd. 118 and after 5.1 km. make a slight right on Ecclestone Dr. After 1.4 km. you will reach the Muskoka River in downtown Bracebridge. There is a trail which shows off both the Upper and Lower Falls.

Now we head for Wilson's Falls (N 45° 3.567' W 79° 18.467'). Continue on Ecclestone which becomes Manitoba St. and after 300m turn right on Taylor Rd. and shortly left on River Rd. In 650 m. continue on Wilsons Falls rd and go 1.5 km to the end. The trails will allow exploration of this fine site.

Our final stop is High Falls (N 45° 5.286' W 79° 18.090'). backtrack on Wilson falls Rd and River Rd and after 2 km. turn left on Taylor Rd. After 1.5 km take the 3rd exit on the roundabout, Cedar Lane. In 4.9 km you will see the entrance to the falls just before ON-11. Park at the end of the road and you will also find Potts and Little High Falls which are next to the High Falls.

This ends our tour.

Haliburton Tour

The Haliburton Tour includes four waterfalls and, of course, they are especially spectacular in fall.

Falls	Page	Rating
Ragged Falls	85	3/4
Long Slide	84	3/4
Ritchie Falls	86	3/4
Elliot Falls	82	3/4

Our first stop is Ragged Falls (N 45° 23.450' W 78° 54.348') found off ON-60 in Ragged Falls PP just west of Algonquin PP. It has a trail which follows the side of this long tumbling falls.

Our second stop is Long Slide (N 45° 15.391' W 78° 51.502'). Go west on ON-60 for 11.6 km and turn left on ON-35. Go south on ON-35 for 15.1 km. and turn left on County Rd 8/Kawagama Lake Rd. where there is a pull off after 2.1 km. Be careful around this trail.

Next stop is Ritchie Falls (N 44° 55.699' W 78° 35.675'). Return to ON-35 and turn left. After 51.1 km turn left on South Lake Rd which continues as County Rd 16. In 7.5 km. turn left on Gelert Rd/County Rd 1 and drive for 2.3 km. Turn right on Ritchie Falls Rd. and you reach the site in 2.1 miles. There is a set of three falls here.

Our final stop is Elliot Falls (N 44° 44.583' W 78° 49.483') Go west on Ritchie Falls Road for 2.1 km and turn left on Gelert Rd/County Rd 1. After 2.3 km turn right on County Rd 16 and drive 7.5 km to ON-35. Turn left on ON-35 and drive 25.1 miles and turn left on Elliot Falls Rd. where you will find the site after 300 m.

This is the end of our tour.

The Bonnechere River Tour

Logging was historically very important along the Bonnechere River. There were obstacles along the river when trying to float the logs and bypasses or chutes were built to allow passage. Our tour will visit the area of these chutes.

Falls	Page	Rating
Bonnechere Falls	122	3/4
Second Chute	126	2/4
Third Chute	127	1/4
Fourth Chute	124	3/4
Fifth Chute	124	1/4

Our first stop is Bonnechere Falls (N 45° 29.933' W 76° 33.65') which used to be called First Chute. From the Town of Refrew, take Hwy 60 East and turn right on Trans-Canada Hwy/ON-17 E. After 2.5 km. turn left at County Road 6 (signs for Lochwinnoch Road), and after another 2.1 km., make a left at Thompson Rd. After about 3.9 km, you will see a parking area on the left. Follow a trail near the back which makes its way down to the river and the falls.

Next we head to Second Chute (N 45° 28.637' W 76° 41.445'). Go southwest on Thompson Rd for 3.9 km and turn right on County Rd 6. After 2.1 km. turn right on ON-17 and proceed for 2.4 km. Turn left on O'Brien Rd/ON-60 and driver 4.3 km where you make a right on Raglan St and park. There is a swinging bridge and the old McDougall Mill by the rocky remnants of second Chute.

Our next stop is Third Chute (N 45°30.466' W 76° 56.15'). Go southwest on Raglan St. and turn right on Bridge St. and then continue on Stewart St. and ON-60. After 21.3 km turn left on Stone St in the town of Douglas and the remnants of the chute are seen shortly.

Our next stop Fourth Chute (N 45° 30.2' W 77°00.42') is a treat for photographers. Head northwest on Stone St. and continue onto Queen St. Shortly turn left on Fourth Chute Rd and drive 6.2 km to the site. There is an upper and lower falls to explore.

The last stop is Fifth Chute (N 45° 32.374' W 77° 05.887') which is really only of historical interest as it has been obliterated by a dam. Turn southwest on Fourth Chute Rd. and continue on Queen St. After 8.1 km turn right on Patrick St/Queen St. and continue on Bridge St. After 0.7 km turn right on Bonnechere St./ON-60and the site is a short distance.

This is the end of our tour.

Northeast Tour

The Northwest Tour involves a double waterfall at North Bay and a wonderful wilderness falls along with a couple of nearby small falls.

Falls	Page	Rating
Duchesnay Falls (West)	131	4/4
Duchesnay Falls (East)	131	4/4
Crooked Chute	130	2/4
Eau Claire Gorge Falls	132	4/4
Peddler's Falls	135	2/4

Our tour begins at the west end of North Bay where we have Duchesnay Falls, East and West (N 46° 20.053' W 79° 30.561'). This is a magnificent set of falls found by ON-17 at North Bay's west end. It is well signed and has an extensive trails that allow you to explore its many sides. Set aside some time for this.

We will now head for one of Ontario's other premier waterfalls but make a short stop on the way to see Crooked Chute (N 46° 16.648' W 78° 55.013'). Take ON-17 east towards Ottawa for 49 km and then turn right on ON-630. In about 1.3 km you will pass over Crooked Chute, small but picturesque and worth stopping for a few minutes.

We will now continue to the wonderful Eau Claire Gorge Falls (N 46° 15.359' W 78° 55.029'). Continue south for another 4 km and turn right on Peddlers drive. Shortly you will see the entrance to Eau Claire Gorge Conservation Area. from the parking area you can take trails to the gorge area and the falls. There are many excellent viewpoints to explore but care is needed here.

As you leave this falls, there is one more small falls nearby, Peddlers Falls (N 46° 15.619' W 78° 50.875'). Return to peddlers Road and head east for about 4.2 km where you cross a bridge. If you look south you will see the falls.

This ends our tour.

Thunder Bay Tour

The Lakehead Region has a lot of top rated waterfalls although some of them are difficult to reach. This tour runs from the Minnesota border past Thunder Bay to Terrace Bay. It would be difficult to do this in one day and still leave time to view these great falls. It would also make a great two day tour from Thunder Bay, going southwest one day and northeast the next.

Falls	Page	Rating
High Falls of the Pigeon River	176	4/4
Middle Falls of the Pigeon River	180	2/4
Kakabeka Falls	178	4/4
Rainbow Falls	180	4/4
Aguasabon Falls	174	4/4

We begin our tour at High Falls of the Pigeon River (N 48° 00.288' W 89° 35.874'). You can access the site from a trail from the Pigeon River Provincial Park but it is easier to cross the border into Minnesota and make an immediate right turn to Grand Portage State Park. from the visitor center a trail runs to the falls and a couple of excellent observation towers.

Our next stop is the Middle Falls of the Pigeon River (N 48° 00.761' W 89° 36.966'). After crossing into Ontario, go 3.1 km north on ON-61 and then left on ON-593. You will see the falls in 2.3 km.

We now head for one of the finest waterfalls in Ontario, Kakabeka Falls (N 48° 24.177' W 89° 37.457'). Return to ON-61 and turn left. Drive 36.8 km and turn left on ON-130, and then after 5.1 km., turn left on Barrie Dr. Proceed for 2.8 km and turn right on River Rd, and then after 5.5 km right on ON-588. Stay on ON-588 for 1.8 km and then turn left on OH-11. After 5.5 km you will have gone through the town of Kakabeka Falls and will see the entrance to Kakabeka Falls Provincial Park. Leave plenty of time for the boardwalk and observation decks on both sides of the falls.

Our next stop is Rainbow Falls (N 48° 50.802' W 87° 23.982'). Go south on ON-11 for 27 km and then turn left on ON-11/ON-17. Drive 191 km and you will see the entrance to Rainbow Falls PP. It is 2 km to the falls from the visitor center.

Our final destination is Aguasabon Falls (N 48° 46.728' W 87° 07.254') Continue east on ON-17 for 23.3 km. and as you reach Terrace Bay, turn right on Aguasabon Gorge Rd and drive to the end where you will find a trail to an observation deck looking over the falls.

The Waterfalls
Niagara Region

Balls Falls Lower,

Niagara Region
Type: Plunge Type
River and County: Twenty Mile Creek, Vineland, Niagara County
GPS Location: N 43° 7.688' W 79° 23.053'
Rating: 4/4
Access: Easy, 5 minutes

Description: This is one of Ontario's finest waterfalls, and, as a bonus, there is another wonderful waterfall nearby, Upper Balls Falls.
Getting There: It can be reached by going north on Highway 24 (Victoria St.) off of Highway 401 Niagara. As you are going up the escarpment, turn left on Sixth Ave, and drive a short way to the parking area. It is well signed.
Photography Tips: The main viewing area near the crest of the falls has a large stone dyke which makes it difficult to get a full shot of the falls. There are a number of places where you can set up in the clear if you look about but be careful because a fall would likely be fatal.

The water flow tends to be low in summer. There is beautiful foliage in the background in fall, and this is an ideal time to visit.

Nearby Attractions: Upper Balls Falls can be reached by trail on the other side of Sixth Ave. and it is a top notch waterfall as well. Along the trail to that falls, you will see the remains of the Balls Woolen Mill, which is very interesting. It is also a good place to get down to water level although you will need to take care.

Balls Falls Upper

Niagara Region
Type: Plunge Type
River and County: Twenty Mile Creek, Vineland, Niagara County
GPS Location: N 43° 7.688' W 79° 23.053'
Rating: 3/4
Access: Moderate, 15 minutes

Description: This is one of two outstanding waterfalls located in the Balls Falls Conservation Area. The Upper Falls has an interesting Karst feature on one side of the gorge, where water flows out of the side of the wall.

Getting There: It can be reached by going north on Highway 24 (Victoria St.) off of Highway 401 Niagara. As you are going up the escarpment, turn left on Sixth Ave, and drive a short way to the parking area. It is well signed.

There are trails on both sides of the creek going upstream. I prefer the north side (your right side looking upstream) as it has the remains of an old mill, Balls Woolen Mill, and it puts you across from the Karst feature. It is also easier to get to river level from this side.

Photography Tips: If you go up the right side you can get excellent photos which include the Karst feature, from both the crest and base of the falls. You will be able to get right next to the falling water. Look also for the remains of the Ball Woolen Mill for some interesting images.

Nearby Attractions: The Lower Balls Falls can be reached from the other side of the highway from this falls. Look also for the Balls Woolen Mills ruin along the trail to the Upper Falls.

Beamer Fall

Niagara Region
Type: Ramp Type
River and County: Forty Mile Creek, Grimsby, Niagara County
GPS Location: N 43° 10.944' W 79° 34.4'
Rating: 3/4
Access: Moderate, 5 Minutes

Description: This is an interesting waterfall found on the Niagara Escarpment above the town of Grimsby, Ontario. It is narrow at the top and widens out towards the bottom
Getting There: Follow Christie south off of the QEW Niagara, and turn right on Ridge Rd. You will find a parking lot on the right about 3/4 mile (1-1/4 km).
Photography Tips: If the sun is out don't bother with this falls in the morning, as it receives a glare on its face. You can take a side view from the trail from the parking lot, and work your way down for some shots from the base. A bit steep, so be careful.
Nearby Attractions: The Beamer Conservation Area is just around the corner which is a great place to watch migrating hawks in the spring. From the conservation parking lot, you can take a trail to Lower Beamer Falls.
There is another nice waterfall downstream from this one, appropriately called Lower Beamer Falls. It is probably easier to reach from the trail from Beamer Conservation Area.

Beamer Falls Lower, Niagara Region, Grimsby
Plunge Type, Forty Mile Creek, Rating: 2/4, Access: Difficult
GPS Location: N 43° 11.013' W 79° 34.211'
From Beamer Cons. Area take trail NE to Creek and go upstream

Beamer Side Falls, Niagara Region, Grimsby
Cascade Type, Trib. Forty Mile Creek, Rating: 1/4, Access: Moderate
GPS Location: N 43° 11.123' W 79° 34.166'
From Beamer Cons. Area take trail NE to Creek and go downstream

Decew Falls Lower, Niagara Region, St. Catharines
Cascade Type, Twenty Mile Creek, Rating: 2/4, Access: Difficult
GPS Location: N 43° 6.617' W 79° 15.816'
Take trail behind Decew Mill to creek level and backtrack upstream

Decew Falls

Niagara Region
Type: Plunge Type
River and County: Twenty Mile Cr., St. Catharines, Niagara County
GPS Location: N 43° 6.617' W 79° 15.816'
Rating: 3/4
Access: Easy, 2 Minutes

Description: This is a gorgeous type of plunge falls with an interesting mill at the top. It is an easy visit for a family outing.

Getting There: To reach Decew Falls from Highway 401 (Niagara) take exit 49 southeast and merge onto King's Hwy 406.Take the St.David's Rd/County Rd-71 exit, merge onto St David's Rd. and turn left at Merrittville Hwy. Take the 1st right onto Decew Rd. There is a parking lot and it is well signed.

The bottom of the gorge can be very difficult to get to. It either involves a dangerous decent near the falls or a long walk along the trail behind the mill to a point where it is safer to descend, and then making your way back upstream to the base of the falls

Photography Tips: There is a classic shot from the base of the falls with the Morningstar Mill at the crest, although it is tough to get to the base. The Mill itself offers some interesting opportunities.

Nearby Attractions: Both Lower Decew Falls and Faucet Falls are nearby, although not easy to access. The Morningstar Mill is at the crest of the Falls.

East 18 Mile Falls, Niagara Region, Jordon
Irregular Cascade Type, Eighteen Mile Creek, Rating: 1/4, Access: Moderate
GPS Location: N 43° 07.583 W 79° 21.274
From 17th St. 1.4 km past top escarpment trail east from pull off

Faucet Falls, Niagara Region, St. Catharines
Plunge Type, Twenty Mile Creek, Rating: 2/4, Access: Difficult
GPS Location: N 43° 6.617' W 79° 15.816'
Take trail behind Decew Mill to creek and go back upstream

Hillside Cascade, Niagara Region, Beamsville
Cascade Type, Bartlett Creek, Rating: 1/4, Access: Private
GPS Location: N 43°9.183' W 79° 27.862'
Permission needed, NW corner of Aberdeen Rd. and Hillside Dr

Louth Falls Upper, Niagara Region, Jordan
Cascade Type, Sixteen Mile Creek, Rating: 1/4, Access: Moderate
GPS Location: N 43° 07.186' W 79° 21.122'
Off Staff Rd. 100 m NE of creek crossing

Louth Falls
Niagara Region
Type: Plunge Type

River and County: Sixteen Mile Creek, Jordan, Niagara County
GPS Location: N 43° 7.448' W 79° 21.016'
Rating: 3/4
Access: Moderate, 30 minutes

Description: While it is not a large waterfall, it is very natural in a pretty
setting. It is also very quiet and peaceful, without a lot of automobile
noise. Well worth a visit and ideal for a family outing.
Getting There: Take Jordan Rd. south off of the QEW Niagara, till you
reach the end. Turn left on Highway 81 and then right on 17th St. Turn
left on Staff Ave, and look for a parking lot on your left. The trail is
part of the Bruce Trail, and a short distance from the parking lot, it
starts down a hill, look for a trail to the left part way down which leads
to the falls.

Photography Tips: While there are many excellent photo opportunities,
I prefer the crest area with some trees and leaves along the bank as a
background. You might like to try setting with a bit higher exposure
than usual, I found this very effective.
Nearby Attractions: Balls Falls and Decew Falls are a short drive.

Lynn Falls, Niagara Region, Norfolk County, Port Dover
Plunge Type, Lynn River, Rating: 1/4, Access: Easy
GPS Location: N 42° 47.910' W 80° 12.804'
Off intersection Prospect and Tisdale Rds north Port Dover

Martins Falls, Niagara Region, Rockway
Plunge Type, Martins Creek, Rating: 1/4, Access: Easy
GPS Location: N 43° 6.672' W 79° 19.224'
Private property, In village Rockway look north from bridge

Middle 18 Mile Falls, Niagara Region, Jordon
Irregular Cascade, Eighteen Mile Creek, Rating: 1/4, Access: Moderate
GPS Location: N 43° 07.583 W 79° 21.274
17th St. 1.4 km past top escarpment trail west from pull off 150 m.

Niagara Falls

Niagara Region
Type: Plunge Type
River and County: Niagara River, Niagara Falls, Niagara County
GPS Location: N 43° 4.736' W 79° 4.528'
Rating: 4/4
Access: Easy, 1 Minute

Description: Millions of words have been written about Niagara Falls, and millions of people have seen its wonders. It is well worth the trip, you will not be disappointed.

Getting There: From the QEW Niagara, take the 420 Exit at Niagara Falls and follow the signs to the falls. Park in one of the many lots and take the shuttle in season.

Photography Tips: This may be the most photographed spot on earth and you will be hard put to find something original. I recommend coming in the dead of winter if you can. There will be only a fraction of the crowds and the snow and ice provide some excellent elements for some great images.

Nearby Attractions: This is one of North America's biggest tourist attractions and there are many things to keep you busy. As well as the wonders of the falls and the rest of the Niagara River, there are a host of places wanting to entertain you in exchange for some of your money.

Rockway Falls

Niagara Region
Type: Ramp Type
River and County: Fifteen Mile Creek, Rockway, Niagara County
GPS Location: N 43° 6.672' W 79° 19.224'
Rating: 4/4
Access: Moderate trail difficulty, walking time

Description: This is a gorgeous waterfalls in a very natural setting. You can get excellent views from the top on both sides of the falls or work your way to the base.

Getting There: If you continue south on Victoria Ave., off of Highway QEW Niagara, past the exit to Balls Falls, you reach the turnoff to Rockway Falls on 8th Ave. Continue to the village of Rockway and park at the community center. A short walk will give you a good view from the top of the falls (Be careful, there are no guardrails). Take the trail behind the community center and you will be able to make your way to the bottom of Fifteen Mile Creek, where you can work your way back to the base of the falls.
Photography Tips: Great views from both the top and base. This falls is especially beautiful in the fall when there is an abundance of colorful foliage.
Nearby Attractions: Have a look on the other side of the bridge for the small but lovely Martins Falls.

Swayze Falls
Niagara Region
Type: Cascade Type
River and County: Twelve Mile Creek, Effingham, Niagara County
GPS Location: N 43° 5.544' W 79° 18.176'
Rating: 3/4
Access: Moderate, 5 Minutes

Description: Located in a very natural woodland setting, it is a great destination for a weekend walk. Summer may not show it at it's best as it can slow to a trickle after a dry spell.

Getting There: To reach Swayze Falls from Highway 401 (Niagara) take exit 49 southeast and merge onto King's Hwy 406.Take the St.David's Rd/County Rd-71 exit, merge onto St David's Rd. and turn left at Merrittville Hwy. Take the 1st right onto Decew Rd. Turn left on Pelham Rd. and proceed 2.3 km (1.8 miles) until a left on Effington Rd. After 3 km. turn left on Roland St and park at the lot at the end. Photography Tips: Even after the best of the fall foliage is past, it can present a great picture with fields of fallen reddish leaves. You can work yourself to the base from the south side with care.
Nearby Attractions: The Decew Falls complex and Morningstar Mill are a few minutes away.

Terrace Falls, Niagara Region, St Catharines
Plunge Type, Terrace Creek, Rating: 2/4, Access: Moderate
GPS Location: N 43° 05.432' W 79° 16.408'
Park at end of Wiley Rd and 1 km south in Short Hills P.P.

Thirty Road Falls, Niagara Region, Beamsville
Cascade Type, Thirty Mile Creek, Rating: 2/4, Access: Moderate
GPS Location: N 43° 10.064' W 79° 30.752'
Take Bruce Trail west from Thirty Road

West 18 Mile Falls, Niagara Region, Jordon
Irregular Cascade Type, Eighteen Mile Creek, Rating: 1/4, Access: Moderate
GPS Location: N 43° 07.583 W 79° 21.274
From 17th St. 1.4 km past top escarpment trail west from pull off 200 m.

Hamilton Region

Albion Falls (Mount Albion Falls)

Hamilton Region
Type: Ramp Type
River and County: Redhill Creek, Hamilton, Hamilton Region
GPS Location: N 43° 12.016' W 79° 49.176'
Rating: 3/4
Access: Moderate, 5 Minutes

Description: Like a couple of Hamilton waterfalls, it has a culvert at the top, but it is not hard to compose a photograph to eliminate or reduce its impact. After a heavy rain or spring melt, it can be very spectacular.
Getting There: Take the eastbound Lincoln Alexander Parkway from Highway 403 in Hamilton and exit at Dartnell Rd and go south (right) make a left on Stone Church Rd. and another left at Pritchard St, and then left on to Mud St. There is a parking lot on the left as you descend the hill and the falls is across the road to the right.
Photography Tips: I think the best shots can be made from the base of the falls which you can reach with a bit of care. There is a rock ledge at the south side of the crest.
Nearby Attractions: Buttermilk Falls is nearby.

Ancaster Heights Falls, Hamilton Region, County, Ancaster
Cascade Type, Trib. of Tiffany Creek, Rating: 1/4, Access: Easy
GPS Location: N 43° 14.412' W 79°57.771'
North side of Wilson St. as it goes down the Niagara Escarpment

Auchmar Falls (Upper Beckett Falls), Hamilton Region, Hamilton
Cascade Type, Unknown River, Rating: 1/4, Access: Moderate
GPS Location: N 43° 14.659' W 79° 53.575'
Off Beckett Dr. 270m north of Auchmar Rd.

Baby Albion Falls, Hamilton Region, Hamilton County, Hamilton
Cascade Type, River, Rating: 1/4, Access: Moderate
GPS Location: N 43° 12.016' W 79° 49.176'
By Mud St., beside Albion Falls

Baby Webster Falls, Hamilton Region, Greensville
Ribbon Type, Spencer Creek Tributary, Rating: 2/4, Access: Easy
GPS Location: N 43° 16.544' W 79° 58.816'
Off Short Rd. in Spencer Gorge Wilderness Area

Beckett Falls (Lower Beckett Falls), Hamilton Region, Hamilton
Cascade Type, Unknown River, Rating: 1/4, Access: Moderate
GPS Location: N 43° 14.688' W 79° 53.364'
Off Beckett Dr., 650 m north of Auchmar Rd.

Betzner Falls (Lower Weir's Falls), Hamilton Region, West
Flamborough
Cascade Type, Trib. Spring Creek, Rating: 2/4, Access: Private
GPS Location: N 43° 15.065' W 80° 00.833'
Located on private property

Billy Green Falls (Battlefield Falls), Hamilton Region, Stoney Creek
Cascade Type, Battlefield Creek, Rating: 2/4, Access: Moderate
GPS Location: N 43° 12.55 W 79° 46.03'
Off Centennial Dr. as it climbs the escarpment

Billy Monkley Cascade, Hamilton Region, Hamilton
Step Type, Not known, Rating: 2/4, Access: Easy
GPS Location: N 43° 12.55' W 79° 46.03'
In Hamilton Conservation Area accessed on Dartnall St

Borer's Falls Lower , Hamilton Region, Clappisons Corners
Cascade Type, Borer's Creek, Rating: 2/4, Access: Difficult
GPS Location: N 43° 17.166' W 79° 56.267'
Difficult descent from Rock Chapel Sanctuary

Borer's Falls (Rock Chapel Falls)

Hamilton Region
Type: Curtain Type
River and County: Rock Chapel Creek, Clappison's Corners, Hamilton
Region
GPS Location: N 43° 17.592' W 79° 56.192'
Rating: 3/4
Access: Easy, 1 Minute

Description: This is a gorgeous falls in all seasons but spectacular in the
fall.
Getting There: Borers Falls can be reached by taking Dundas St.
(Highway 5) west off of Highway 6 just north of Hamilton. Turn left
on Rock Chapel Rd. and go for about 1 mile (1.6 km.) You will come
to a bridge with small parking lots on both sides to the left.
Photography Tips: There are trails on both sides of the falls which
offer excellent setup spots for images.

Nearby Attractions: These falls are close to nearby Websters and Tews Falls which are both better known but Borers is spectacular in its own right.

Boundary Falls, Hamilton Region, Waterdown
Plunge Type, Grindstone Tributary, Rating: 2/4, Access: Difficult
GPS Location: N 43° 19.567' W 79° 53.267'
Off Mill St. in Waterdown opposite to the water treatment plant

Broman Falls, Hamilton Region, Hamilton
Cascade Type, Not known, Rating: 2/4, Access: Moderate
GPS Location: N 43° 12.784' W 79° 49.027'
Off the Rail Trail on the west side of Mohawk Rd.

Brown Falls, Hamilton Region, Waterdown
Ribbon Type, Grindstone Creek tributary, Rating: 2/4, Access: Easy
GPS Location: N 43° 20.196' W 79° 53.250'
Off George St in Waterdown

Buttermilk Falls, Hamilton Region, Town
Plunge Type, Trib. Of Redhill Cr., Rating: 2/4, Access: Easy
GPS Location: N 43° 12.306' W 79° 49.188'
Off Mountain Brow Blvd just past Mud St.

Canterbury Falls (**Milne Falls**), Hamilton Region, Ancaster
Cascade Type, Canterbury Creek, Rating: 2/4, Access: Easy
GPS Location: N 43° 14.064' W 79° 58.411'
10 minutes on Bruce Trail from Ancaster Old Mill

Cave Falls, Hamilton Region, Hamilton
Cascade Type, Trib. Redhill Cr., Rating: 1/4, Access: Difficult
GPS Location: N 43° 12.366' W 79° 48.804'
Downstream from Buttermilk Falls on south side of ravine

Centennial Falls, Hamilton Region, Stoney Creek
Ribbon Type, Trib. Battlefield Creek, Rating: 1/4, Access: Difficult
GPS Location: N 43° 12.522' W 79° 46.080'
May be private property, Off Centennial Dr.

Chedoke Falls Lower

Hamilton Region
Type: Curtain Type
River and County: Chedoke Creek, Hamilton, Hamilton Region
GPS Location: N 43° 14.554' W 79° 54.032'
Rating: 3/4
Access: Difficult, 30 Minutes

Description: Chedoke Falls is memorable for having an interesting turquoise colour to the water as well as its interesting layered and colored rock sides.

Getting There: It is reached from the intersection of Scenic Drive and Denlow Ave. From the culvert on the south side, follow a rough trail on the east side. After you have reached the bottom, you will see Chedoke Falls to your left. If you proceed downstream you will reach Lower Chedoke Falls after about 20 minutes. There is no real trail. You can also come upstream from the Chedoke Trail. Suitable footwear is a must.

Photography Tips: Your hard work in reaching this falls will be rewarded by a very picturesque falls in a natural scene. Good images are available from the bottom as well as the crest. Note the turquoise water colour.

Nearby Attractions: Chedoke Falls is upstream, you will note it if you have come in from Scenic Drive and Denlow Ave.

Chedoke Falls

Hamilton Region
Type: Curtain Type
River and County: Chedoke Creek, Hamilton, Hamilton Region
GPS Location: N 43° 14.554' W 79° 54.032'
Rating: 3/4
Access: Difficult, 10 Minutes

Description: Chedoke Falls is memorable for having an interesting turquoise colour to the water as well as its interesting layered and colored rock sides.
Getting There: It is reached from the intersection of Scenic Drive and Denlow Ave. From the culvert on the south side, follow a rough trail on the east side. Be careful, it can be steep in spots and it would be easy to fall. Suitable footwear is a must.

Photography Tips: The difficulty in reaching this falls is rewarded with a multitude of interesting aspects for the photographer. Incorporate the walls and water colour for interesting images.

Nearby Attractions: Lower Chedoke Falls is downstream, a difficult bushwhack but worth it.

Clappison Falls, Hamilton Region, Hamilton
Cascade Type, Unknown source, Rating: 1/4, Access: Easy
GPS Location: N 43° 18.485' W 79° 54.747'
Off Highway 6 north of Highway 403

Cliffview Falls Lower, Hamilton Region, Hamilton
Cascade Type, Chedoke Creek, Rating: 2/4, Access: Difficult
GPS Location: N 43° 14.717' W 79° 54.5'
By stairs going up escarpment at end of Beddoe Cr.

Cliffview Falls, Hamilton Region, Hamilton
Cascade Type, Chedoke Creek, Rating: 2/4, Access: Difficult
GPS Location: N 43° 14.717' W 79° 54.5'
By top stairs going up escarpment at end of Beddoe Cr.

Darnley Cascade (Stutts Falls), Hamilton Region, Greensville
Step Type, Spencer Creek, Rating: 2/4, Access: Easy
GPS Location: N 43° 16.704' W 80° 0.224'
Off Harvest Rd. at Crooks Hollow Conservation Area

Deal Cascade, Hamilton Region, Stoney Creek
Cascade Type, Unknown River, Rating: 1/4, Access: Private
GPS Location: N 43° 11.734' W 79° 38.638'
On private property, Bruce Trail north of Fifty Road

Denlow Falls, Hamilton Region, Hamilton
Curtain Type, Chedoke Creek, Rating: 1/4, Access: Difficult
GPS Location: N 43° 14.554' W 79° 54.032'
Below the intersection of Denlow Ave and Scenic Dr.

Devil's Punchbowl Lower, Hamilton Region, Stoney Creek
Curtain Type, Stoney Creek, Rating: 2/4, Access: Moderate
GPS Location: N 43° 12.592' W 79° 45.32'
Off Ridge Rd in Stoney Creek

Devil's Punchbowl (Horseshoe Falls)

Hamilton Region
Type: Ribbon Type
River and County: Stoney Creek, Stoney Creek, Hamilton Region
GPS Location: N 43° 12.592' W 79° 45.32'
Rating: 3/4
Access: Easy, 2 Minutes

Description: The Devil's Punch Bowl is an unusually well shaped waterfall which falls over the Niagara escarpment. It is often no more than a trickle as it has a small area of drainage, but can be impressive after a few days of rain.

Getting There: To reach it, take Centennial Parkway (Highway20) south off of the QEW Niagara, and follow it up the escarpment to Ridge Rd. on the left. Follow this road a short way around a bend and you will find a parking area on the left. You can also access a trail at the bend which will allow you to access the bottom of the falls, and you will pass a smaller falls on the way.
Photography Tips: From the south edge, you can get some nice views and there are often flowers that can be used in the foreground. Images from the base will show interesting and colorful rock layers.

Nearby Attractions: The Lower Devils Punchbowl is a short distance downstream from this falls.

Dewitt Falls, Hamilton Region, Stoney Creek
Curtain Type, Unknown source, Rating: 2/4, Access: Easy
GPS Location: N 43° 12.252' W 79° 43'
Beside Dewitt Rd at top of escarpment

Duchess Falls, Hamilton Region, Town
Cascade Type, Lang's Creek, Rating: 1/4, Access: Moderate
GPS Location: N 43° 14.8' W 79° 55.783'
End of Ewan, across green space to under Hwy 403

Dundas Falls, Hamilton Region, Dundas
Plunge Type, Spencer Creek, Rating: 2/4, Access: Easy
GPS Location: N 43° 16.5' W 79° 58.32'
Off King St. W in Dundas after Head St.

Dyment Falls, Hamilton Region, Dundas
Curtain Type, Spencer Creek Tributary, Rating: 2/4, Access: Easy
GPS Location: N 43° 16.663' W 79° 56.992'
Top of Sydenham St., take trail from lookout

East Glover's Falls, Hamilton Region, Hamilton
Cascade Type, Davis Creek, Rating: 1/4, Access: Moderate
GPS Location: N 43° 12.540' W 79° 46.446'
From Greenhill Rd. take trail behind Water Treatment Plant

East Iroquoia Falls, Hamilton Region, Hamilton
Cascade Type, Unknown River, Rating: 1/4, Access: Easy
GPS Location: N 43° 14.667' W 79° 56.4'
View from White Chapel Cemetery off Old Ancaster Rd.

Erland Falls, Hamilton Region, Stoney Creek
Cascade Type, Unknown River, Rating: 1/4, Access: Easy
GPS Location: N 43° 12.252' W 79° 43'
From Dewitt Rd, take track allowance west and see on right side.

Felker's Falls

Hamilton Region
Type: Curtain Type
River and County: Redhill Creek, Hamilton, Hamilton Region
GPS Location: N 43° 12.192' W 79° 47.384'
Rating: 3/4
Access: Easy, 5 Minutes

Description: Felker's is found in a very natural setting although the easy trail at the crest provides only a distant view.

Getting There: From the Highway 403, take the Lincoln Alexander Expressway and get off on the Mud St Exit. Make a left on Paramount Dr. and a right on Ackland St. You will find a small park where you can leave your car, and take the trail east for about ten minutes.

Photography Tips: The view is a bit distant but the trees surrounding the falls are very nice. Look for a couple of open areas free from obstructing branches.

Nearby Attractions: Albion Falls is a short drive away.

Ferguson Falls, Hamilton Region, Greensville
Cascade Type, Logie's Creek, Rating: 2/4, Access: Difficult
GPS Location: N 43° 16.794' W 79° 58.602'
Private

Fifty Road Cascade, Hamilton Region, Stoney Creek
Cascade Type, Unknown River, Rating: 1/4, Access: Easy
GPS Location: N 43° 11.734' W 79° 38.638'
Above the Bruce Trail east of Fifty Road

Fruitland Falls Lower, Hamilton Region, Stoney Creek
Cascade Type, Unknown River, Rating: 1/4, Access: Easy
GPS Location: N 43° 12.252' W 79° 43'
From the top end of Dewitt Rd go east along the rail allowance

Fruitland Falls Upper, Hamilton Region, Stoney Creek
Cascade Type, Unknown River, Rating: 1/4, Access: Easy
GPS Location: N 43° 12.252' W 79° 43'
From the top end of Dewitt Rd go east along the rail allowance

Glendale Falls Lower, Hamilton Region, Hamilton
Cascade Type, Trib. Redhill Creek, Rating: 2/4, Access: Moderate
GPS Location: N 43° 12.15' W 79° 48.833'
Take trail at end of Kingsview Dr.

Glendale Falls Middle (Glendale Cascade), Hamilton
Cascade Type, Trib. Redhill Creek, Rating: 2/4, Access: Difficult
GPS Location: N 43° 12.15' W 79° 48.833'
Take trail at end of Kingsview Dr.

Glendale Falls Upper (Glendale Falls), Hamilton Region, Hamilton
Cascade Type, Trib. Redhill Creek, Rating: 2/4, Access: Difficult
GPS Location: N 43° 12.15' W 79° 48.833'
Take trail at end of Kingsview Dr.

Glover's Falls, Hamilton Region, Hamilton
Cascade Type, Davis Creek, Rating: 1/4, Access: Moderate
GPS Location: N 43° 12.530' W 79° 46.458'
From Greenhill Rd. take trail behind Water Treatment Plant

Grand Cascade, Hamilton Region, Stoney Creek
Cascade Type, Trib. Fifty Creek, Rating: 1/4, Access: Moderate
GPS Location: N 43° 11.734' W 79° 38.638'
Above Bruce Trail west of Fifty Road

Great Falls (Grindstone Falls, Waterdown Falls, Smokey Hollow Falls)

Hamilton Region
Type: Plunge Type
River and County: Grindstone Creek, Hamilton County
GPS Location: N 43° 19.8 W 79° 53.233
Rating: 3/4

Access: Easy, 1 minute

Description: This falls provided the power for mills in this area, remnants of which can be seen near the base. The area was an early industrial center and came to be known as Smokey Hollow. Low water levels caused their end in the early part of the 20th century.

Getting There: Go south on Mill St. in Waterdown, from the Highway 5 intersection (Dundas St.) As you go down a hill to the left, you will see the small parking lot on your right. A short walk down the gentle slope brings you to a platform beside the top of the falls. Another short walk south brings you to the Bruce Trail where you can descend to the base level of the falls.

Photography Tips: After descending to below the falls on the Bruce Trail, you can move back upstream to the base of the falls. There are some interesting boulders and the remains of an old mill that you can use in your shots. In the winter, there are excellent ice features as well. You need to be careful getting to the base, especially in winter.

Nearby Attractions: Walking down the Bruce Trail in this location is beautiful in all seasons, and a fifteen minute walk brings you to Grindstone Cascade. Nearby you will find Spring, Brown's, James, Hidden Grindstone, Boundary, and Upper and Lower Snake Falls.

Greensville Falls, Hamilton Region, Greensville
Cascade Type, Greensville Creek, Rating: 1/4, Access: Easy
GPS Location: N 43° 16.8' W 79° 59.517'
Off Crooks Hollow Rd in Conservation Area trail

Grindstone Cascade, Hamilton Region, Waterdown
Cascade Type, Grindstone Creek, Rating: 2/4, Access: Moderate
GPS Location: N 43° 19.75' W 79° 53.25'
Bruce Trail from Mill St in Waterdown

Hannon Cascade, Hamilton Region, Town
Step Type, Unknown River, Rating: 2/4, Access: Easy
GPS Location: N 43° 11.276' W 79° 49.740'
Off Rymal Rd between Dartnall and Pritchard Rds.

Heritage Falls (Griffin Falls), Hamilton Region, Ancaster
Step Type, Trib. Sulphur Creek, Rating: 2/4, Access: Easy
GPS Location: N 43° 14.933' W 79° 59.567'
Off Homestead Trail from Mineral Springs Rd.

Heritage Green Falls, Hamilton Region, Hamilton
Washboard Type, Trib. Upper Davis Creek, Rating: 1/4 Access: Easy
GPS Location: N 43° 12.282' W 79° 47.250'
Follow Peter St. trail from Felker's Falls CA

Hermitage Cascade (Hermitage Falls), Hamilton Region, Ancaster
Cascade Type, Hermitage Creek, Rating: 2/4, Access: Easy
GPS Location: N 43° 14.933' W 79° 59.567'
Behind gatehouse at Hermitage off Sulphur Springs Road

Hidden Grindstone Falls, Hamilton Region, Waterdown
Cascade Type, Trib. Grindstone Creek, Rating: 1/4, Access: Private
GPS Location: N 43° 19.668' W 79° 53.256'
West side of Grindstone Creek, Private

Hopkins Cascade Lower, Hamilton Region, Dundas
Cascade Type, Hopkins Creek, Rating: 1/4, Access: Moderate
GPS Location: N 43° 17.802' W 79° 55.229'
Bruce Trail west of Valley Road

Hopkins Cascade Upper, Hamilton Region, Dundas
Cascade Type, Hopkins Creek, Rating: 1/4, Access: Difficult
GPS Location: N 43° 17.802' W 79° 55.229'
Bruce Trail west of Valley Road

Hunter Falls, Hamilton Region, Troy
Cascade Type, Hunter Creek, Rating: 2/4, Access: Private
GPS Location: N 43° 16.116' W 80° 10.617'
Off Hunter Rd, Private but can be seen from road

James Falls, Hamilton Region, Waterdown
Ribbon Type, Trib. Grindstone Creek, Rating: 1/4, Access: Private
GPS Location: N 43° 20.172' W 79° 53.268'
Private

Jones Road Falls, Hamilton Region, Stoney Creek
Cascade Type, Unknown River, Rating: 1/4, Access: Moderate
GPS Location: N 43° 12.351' W 79° 41.711'
Below Bruce Trail wet of Jones Rd. Access

Lafarge Falls, Hamilton Region, Dundas
Ribbon Type, Trib. Sydenham Creek, Rating: 1/4, Access: Private
GPS Location: N 43° 16.616' W 79° 57.516'
On private property

Lewis Road East Falls, Hamilton Region, Stoney Creek
Cascade Type, Unknown River, Rating: 1/4, Access: Moderate
GPS Location: N 43° 12.282' W 79° 39.790'
On the south side of the Bruce Trail east of McNeilly Rd

Lewis Road West Falls, Hamilton Region, Stoney Creek
Cascade Type, Unknown River, Rating: 1/4, Access: Moderate
GPS Location: N 43° 12.282' W 79° 39.790'
On the south side of the Bruce Trail east of McNeilly Rd

Little Canterbury Falls, Hamilton Region, Ancaster
Cascade Type, Trib. Canterbury Creek, Rating: 2/4, Access: Easy
GPS Location: N 43° 14.064' W 79° 58.411
10 minutes on the Bruce Trail from Ancaster Old Mill

Little Davis Falls, Hamilton Region, Stoney Creek
Curtain Type, Davis Creek, Rating: 2/4, Access: Easy
GPS Location: N 43° 12.30' W 79° 47.266'
Trail from end of Quigley Rd.

Little Falls Lower on Wilson, Hamilton Region, Ancaster
Cascade Type, Ancaster Creek Trib., Rating: 1/4, Access: Easy
GPS Location: N 43° 14.4' W 79°57.783'
Below Wilson St as it goes down the escarpment

Little Falls on Wilson, Hamilton Region, Ancaster
Cascade Type, Ancaster Creek Trib., Rating: 2/4, Access: Easy
GPS Location: N 43° 14.4' W 79°57.783'
Above Wilson St as it goes down the escarpment

Little Rock Chapel Falls (**Rock Chapel Road Falls**), Hamilton
Region, Dundas
Ribbon Type, Unknown River, Rating: 1/4, Access: Difficult
GPS Location: N 43° 17.333' W 79° 56.301'
Below Bruce Trail north of Rock Chapel Road Access

Lower Mills Falls, Hamilton Region, Ancaster
Curtain Type, Ancaster Creek, Rating: 2/4, Access: Easy
GPS Location: N 43° 13.993' W 79° 58.467'
At Ancaster Old Mill at 548 Old Dundas Rd.

Lower Sydenham Falls, Hamilton Region, Dundas
Curtain Type, River, Rating: 2/4, Access: Moderate
GPS Location: N 43° 16.483' W 79° 57.516'
Bruce Trail from Sydenham St north of Crowley Crt.

McNeilly Falls, Hamilton Region, Stoney Creek
Cascade Type, Unknown River, Rating: 2/4, Access: Moderate
GPS Location: N 43° 12.142' W 79° 40.567'
Located just north of the hairpin at the top of McNeilly Rd

Middle Sydenham Falls, Hamilton Region, Dundas
Curtain Type, River, Rating: 2/4, Access: Moderate
GPS Location: N 43° 16.5' W 79° 57.516'
Bruce Trail from Sydenham St north of Crowley Crt.

Mineral Springs Falls, Hamilton Region, Mineral Springs,
Cascade Type, Sulphur Creek, Rating: 2/4, Access: Easy
GPS Location: N 43° 14.28' W 80° 00.03'
Off Sulphur Springs Rd north of Mineral Springs Rd.

Mountain Spring Falls, Hamilton Region, Stoney Creek
Cascade Type, Trib. Davis Creek, Rating: 1/4, Access: Moderate
GPS Location: N 43° 12.30' W 79° 47.266'
Take trail south from end of Quigley Rd.

Mountview Falls, Hamilton Region, Hamilton
Cascade Type, Trib. Chedoke River, Rating: 1/4, Access: Easy
GPS Location: N 43° 14.767' W 79° 55.3'
Go east on Chedoke Radial Trail from Scenic Rd entrance

Oak Knoll Falls, Hamilton Region, Hamilton
Cascade Type, Unknown River, Rating: 1/4, Access: Easy
GPS Location: N 43° 12.361' W 79° 49.003'
North end of Oak Knoll Park on Mountain Brow Boulevard

Old Dundas Road Falls, Hamilton Region, Ancaster
Ribbon type, Ancaster Creek, Rating: 2/4, Access: private
GPS Location: N 43° 14.3' W 79° 58.383'
On private property but viewable from Bruce Trail by Old Dundas Rd

Optimist Cascade, Hamilton Region, Dundas
Cascade Type, Spencer Creek Trib., Rating: 1/4, Access: Easy
GPS Location: N 43° 16.692' W 79° 59.244'
Optimist Park off Brock Rd south of Harvest Rd.

Patterson East Cascade, Hamilton Region, Dundas
Cascade Type, Unknown source, Rating: 1/4, Access: Easy
GPS Location: N 43° 17.855' W 79° 55.667'
Off Patterson Rd just east of Valley Rd.

Patterson West Cascade, Hamilton Region, Dundas
Cascade Type, Unknown source, Rating: 1/4, Access: Easy
GPS Location: N 43° 17.855' W 79° 55.667'
Off Patterson Rd just east of Valley Rd.

Pond Falls Lower, Hamilton Region, Stoney Creek
Ribbon Type, Unknown source, Rating: 1/4, Access: Private
GPS Location: N 43° 12.282' W 79° 39.790'
Below Bruce Trail between McNeilly Rd and Fifty Rd

Pond Falls, Hamilton Region, Stoney Creek
Ribbon Type, Unknown source, Rating: 1/4, Access: Moderate
GPS Location: N 43° 12.282' W 79° 39.790'
Above Bruce Trail between McNeilly Rd and Fifty Rd

Princess Falls Lower (Lang's Falls), Hamilton Region, Hamilton
Cascade Type, Lang's Creek, Rating: 2/4, Access: Easy
GPS Location: N 43° 14.75' W 79° 55.733'
Above Highway 403 as it climbs the escarpment

Princess Falls Upper , Hamilton Region, Hamilton
Ribbon Type, Lang's Creek, Rating: 2/4, Access: Easy
GPS Location: N 43° 14.75' W 79° 55.733'
Above Highway 403 along Chedoke Rail Trail

Pritchard Falls , Hamilton Region, Hamilton
Ribbon Type, Surface water, Rating: 1/4, Access: Easy
GPS Location: N 43° 12.066' W 79° 48.978'
Red Hill Trail from Mud St just east Pritchard Rd.

Progrestron Falls, Hamilton Region, Hamilton

Curtain Type, Twelve Mile Creek, Rating: 2/4, Access: private
GPS Location: N 43° 23.833' W 79° 57.55'
Private, Off Progreston Rd 1.4 km north of Center Rd

Promontory Falls, Hamilton Region, Stoney Creek
Ribbon Type, River, Rating: 1/4, Access: Moderate
GPS Location: N 43° 12.282' W 79° 39.790'
South side of Bruce Trail west of McNeilly Rd.

Ridge Falls, Hamilton Region, Stoney Creek
Cascade Type, Unknown River, Rating: 2/4, Access: Easy
GPS Location: N 43° 12.252' W 79° 43'
Park at the top of Dewitt Rd and go east along the rail allowance

Sanatorium Cascade Lower (Lower Sanatorium Falls), Hamilton Region, Hamilton
Cascade Type, Trib. Chedoke Creek, Rating: 2/4, Access: Moderate
GPS Location: N 43° 14.754' W 79° 54.888'
Off Chedoke Radial Trail west of Beddoe Dr. Access

Sanatorium Falls (Upper Sanatorium Falls, Sanatorium Ravine),
Hamilton Region, Hamilton
Cascade Type, Trib. Chedoke Creek, Rating: 1/4, Access: Easy
GPS Location: N 43° 14.556' W 79° 54.906'
Off Sanatorium Rd north of Scenic Dr.

Scenic Falls, Hamilton Region, Hamilton
Cascade Type, River unknown, Rating: 2/4, Access: Moderate
GPS Location: N 43° 14.65' W 79° 56.07'
Along Chedoke Radial Trail west of Scenic Rd entrance

Shaver Falls Upper (Upper Filman Falls), Hamilton Region,
Ancaster
Cascade Type, Trib. Ancaster Creek, Rating: 2/4, Access: Private
GPS Location: N 43° 14.276' W 79° 57.013'
Private property

Shaver Falls (Filman Falls), Hamilton Region, Ancaster
Ribbon Type, Trib. Ancaster Creek, Rating: 2/4, Access: Moderate
GPS Location: N 43° 14.563' W 79° 56.841'
From Filman Rd follow Bruce Trail and keep left

Sherman Falls (Fairy Falls, Angel Falls)

Hamilton Region
Type: Curtain Type (Two drops)
River and County: Ancaster Creek, Ancaster, Hamilton Region
GPS Location: N 43° 14.3' W 79° 58.383'
Rating: 3/4
Access: Easy, 2 Minutes

Description: This is a great destination in the Hamilton region, and a waterfall that is worth a visit in any season. There is a boardwalk which brings you to the base of the falls.
Getting There: Take the Mohawk exit to Ancaster off of Highway 403, right on Wilson St., then left on Montgomery Drive. Turn right on Old Dundas Rd, and park near the next intersection. Trails to the falls will be on your left.
Photography Tips: It is any easy matter to approach the base of the falls from both sides of the creek. Look for an interesting piece of wood on the right side. A great winter waterfall.
Nearby Attractions: Tiffany Falls is nearby.

Sisters of Mary Falls (Upper Canterbury Falls), Hamilton Region, Ancaster
Cascade Type, Trib. Sulphur Creek, Rating: 2/4, Access: Moderate
GPS Location: N 43° 13.902' W 79° 58.917'
Heritage Trail from Ancaster Old Mill and off trail at bend

Spring Falls (Upper Grindstone Falls, Arnolds Falls), Hamilton Region, Waterdown
Curtain Type, Spring Creek, Rating: 2/4, Access: Easy
GPS Location: N 43° 20.183' W 79° 53.233'
Off George St., private but view from public rd.

Springhill Falls, Hamilton Region, Dundas
Cascade Type, Unknown source, Rating: 1/4, Access: Easy
GPS Location: N 43° 16.251' W 79° 58.936'
On Hwy 8 west of Dundas

Stephanie Falls, Hamilton Region, Hamilton
Cascade Type, Tiffany Creek, Rating: 2/4, Access: Private
GPS Location: N 43° 23.287' W 79° 95.699'
Private Property

Steven's Falls, Hamilton Region, West Flamborough
Cascade Type, Trib. Spring Creek, Rating: 1/4, Access: Difficult
GPS Location: N 43° 15.618' W 80° 01.416'
Off east side of Middleton rd between #154 and 144

Tallman East Falls (Vinemount East Falls), Hamilton Region,
Stoney Creek
Plunge Type, Unknown source, Rating: 1/4, Access: Moderate
GPS Location: N 43° 12.146' W 79° 40.358'
Off Bruce Trail west from McNeilly Road

Tallman West Falls (Shed Falls), Hamilton Region, Stoney Creek
Ribbon Type, Unknown source, Rating: 1/4, Access: Moderate
GPS Location: N 43° 12.351' W 79° 41.711'
Above Bruce Trail west from McNeilly Road on private property

Tews Falls Lower (Baby Tews Falls, Hopkins Ravine), Hamilton
Region, Greensville
Curtain Type, Logie's Creek, Rating: 2/4, Access: Difficult
GPS Location: N 43° 16.692' W 79° 58.608'
Trail from Woodley Lane in Dundas

Tew's Falls (Hopkin's Falls)

Hamilton Region
Type: Ribbon Type
River and County: Logie's Creek, Greensville, Hamilton Region
GPS Location: N 43° 16.85' W 79° 58.6'
Rating: 3/4
Access: Easy, 5 Minutes

Description: This is a gorgeous falls, large and in a beautiful setting especially in the fall.
Getting There: Tew's Falls is only a short way from Websters Falls. Take Brock Rd. south off of Highway 5, turn left onto Harvest Rd. and continue .6km past Short Rd. to a parking lot on the right.
Photography Tips: The observation platform to one side is an excellent set up point. With difficulty, you can also make your way to the base of the falls.
Nearby Attractions: Webster's Falls is only a few minutes away.

Thomas Falls (West of Fifty Lower Falls), Hamilton, Stoney Creek
Cascade Type, Unknown source, Rating: 2/4, Access: Moderate
GPS Location: N 43° 11.934' W 79° 38.886'
Below Bruce Trail west of Fifty Rd.

Tiffany Falls

Hamilton Region
Type: Cascade Type
River and County: Tiffany Creek, Ancaster, Hamilton Region
GPS Location: N 43° 14.436' W 79° 57.594'
Rating: 3/4
Access: Easy, 5 Minutes

Description: A great place for a family outing, the recently renovated trail makes it easy for everyone to walk in.
Getting There: A newly renovated trail provides easy access to this lovely waterfall between Dundas and Ancaster, Ontario. To reach it, take the Mohawk exit fro Highway 403 towards Ancaster and turn right at Wilson St. E. As you get near the bottom of the hill, look to your right to the signed parking lot for the trail beginning.
Photography Tips: This is one of the nicest winter waterfalls with delicate ice crystals like lace. Try a photo shoot in the winter.
Nearby Attractions: Sherman Falls is nearby.

Troy Falls, Hamilton Region, Troy
Cascade Type, Not Known, Rating: 2/4, Access: Private
GPS Location: N 43° 15.667' W 80° 10.683'
Private but viewable from Reg Rd 5 in Troy

Upper Mills Falls, Hamilton Region, Ancaster
Curtain Type, Ancaster Creek, Rating: 2/4, Access: Easy
GPS Location: N 43° 13.993' W 79° 58.467'
At Ancaster Old Mill at 548 Old Dundas Rd.
Upper Sydenham Falls, Hamilton Region, Dundas
Curtain Type, River, Rating: 2/4, Access: Moderate
GPS Location: N 43° 16.616' W 79° 57.516'
Bruce Trail from Sydenham St north of Crowley Crt.

Valley Falls, Hamilton Region, Dundas
Plunge Type, Unknown source, Rating: 1/4, Access: Moderate
GPS Location: N 43° 17.855' W 79° 55.667'
East of Valley Rd from 100 m south of Patterson Rd.

Veever's Falls, Hamilton Region, Hamilton
Cascade Type, Unknown, Rating: 1/4, Access: Moderate
GPS Location: N 43° 12.577' W 79° 46.905'
Follow Bruce Trail from access across from 743 Greenhill Ave.

Vinemount East Falls (Vinemount Middle Falls), Hamilton Region, Stoney Creek
Ribbon Type, Unknown source, Rating: 1/4, Access: Easy
GPS Location: N 43° 12.146' W 79° 40.358'
Above Bruce Trail 0.5 km west of McNeilly Rd

Vinemount West Falls, Hamilton Region, Stoney Creek
Ribbon Type, Unknown source, Rating: 1/4, Access: Easy
GPS Location: N 43° 12.351' W 79° 41.711'
Above Bruce Trail 1 km west of McNeilly Rd

Wall Falls, Hamilton Region, Stoney Creek
Karst/ Cascade Type, Unknown River, Rating: 1/4, Access: Easy
GPS Location: N 43° 12.252' W 79° 43'
From the top of Dewitt Rd go east along the rail allowance

Walnut Grove Falls, Hamilton Region, Hamilton
Ribbon Type, ground water, Rating: 1/4, Access: private
GPS Location: N 43° 12.078' W 79° 49.038'
Private

Washboard Falls (Upper Tiffany Falls), Hamilton Region, Ancaster
Type: Cascade Type, Tiffany Creek, 3/4, Private
GPS Location: N 43° 14.317' W 79° 57.5'
Access: Private
Description: This is a very interesting falls. The structure is due to the fact that the individual rock layers are evenly eroded.
Photography Tips: This falls is on private property and you need permission to visit. As of this writing this permission is not likely to be received.
Nearby Attractions: Tiffany and Sherman Falls are nearby.

Webster's Falls (Fisher's Falls, Flamborough Falls, Hatt's Falls, Spencer's Falls)

Hamilton Region
Type: Curtain Type
River and County: Spencer Creek, Greensville, Hamilton Region
GPS Location: N 43° 16.544' W 79° 58.816'
Rating: 4/4
Access: Easy, 2 Minutes

Description: My favorite Hamilton Region waterfall, it is interesting in all seasons. Easily accessed and a great place for a family outing.
Getting There: You can reach this area by taking Brock Rd. south off of Highway 5. Turn left onto Harvest Rd, and then right onto Short Rd, which will shortly lead you to parking for the conservation area.
Photography Tips: You can get near the crest and their are stairs that will bring you to the base. Additionally there are good vantage pints on the ridge across from the falls, look for a walkway to there.
Nearby Attractions: Tew's Falls is nearby. Look for Baby Webster Falls as you descend the stairs
Note: The stairs were closed for repairs and may not be open.

Weir's Falls (Upper Weir's Falls), Hamilton Region, West
Flamborough
Ribbon Type, Trib. Spring Creek, Rating: 2/4, Access: Private
GPS Location: N 43° 15.727' W 80° 00.646'
Private but visible from Weir's Lane

West Iroquoia Falls, Hamilton Region, Hamilton
Cascade Type, Unknown River, Rating: 1/4, Access: Easy
GPS Location: N 43° 14.667' W 79° 56.4'
View from White Chapel Cemetery off Old Ancaster Rd.

West McNeilly Falls, Hamilton Region, Stoney Creek
Cascade Type, Unknown River, Rating: 1/4, Access: Moderate
GPS Location: N 43° 12.146' W 79° 40.358'
Located south Bruce Trail west of McNeilly Rd

West of Fifty Cascade (West of Fifty Upper Cascade), Hamilton
Region, Stoney Creek
Cascade Type, Unknown source, Rating: 2/4, Access: Moderate
GPS Location: N 43° 11.734' W 79° 38.638'
Above Bruce Trail just west of Fifty Rd.

Westcliffe Falls Lower, Hamilton Region, Hamilton
Cascade Type, Chedoke Creek, Rating: 2/4, Access: Difficult
GPS Location: N 43° 14.717' W 79° 54.5'
By stairs going up escarpment at end of Beddoe Cr.

Westcliffe Falls, Hamilton Region, Hamilton
Ribbon Type, Trib. Chedoke Creek, Rating: 2/4, Access: Difficult
GPS Location: N 43° 14.670' W 79° 54.468'
West of top stairs going up escarpment at end of Beddoe Cr.

Winona Falls (East of Fifty Falls), Hamilton Region, Stoney Creek
Curtain Type, Fifty Creek, Rating: 1/4, Access: Moderate
GPS Location: N 43° 11.667' W 79° 38.417'
Above the Bruce Trail east of Fifty Road

South Central Region

Bruce County

Barrows Bay Falls, South Central Region, Bruce County, Barrows Bay
Irregular Cascade Type, Judge's Creek, Rating: 1/4, Access: Easy
GPS Location: N 44° 57.582' W 81° 13.590'
Off W Shore Rd in Barrows Bay

Colpoys Falls, South Central Region, Bruce County, Colpoys Bay
Irregular cascade Type, Colpoys Creek, Rating: 1/4, Access: Private
GPS Location: N 44° 46.968' W 81° 07.518'
Private but viewable from Krib's Road

Cypress Lake Outlet Falls, South Central Region, Bruce County,
Cypress Lake
Step Type, Cypress Lake, Rating: 1/4, Access: Easy
GPS Location: N 45° 14.184' W 81° 31.566'
End of Cyprus Lake Road Dr. past the campgrounds

Sauble Falls, South Central Region, Bruce County, Sauble Beach
Cascade Type, Sauble River, Rating: 2/4, Access: Easy
GPS Location: N 44° 40.567' W 81° 15.333'
Off Bruce Rd 13 north of Sauble Beach

Dufferin County

Canning Falls Lower, South Central Region, Dufferin County,
Camilla
Plunge Type, Nottawasaga River, Rating: 2/4, Access: Private
GPS Location: N 59° 16.244' W 80° 57.089'
Private property just outside of the Hockley Valley Nature Reserve

Canning Falls Upper, South Central Region, Dufferin County,
Camilla
Plunge Type, Nottawasaga River, Rating: 2/4, Access: Private
GPS Location: N 59° 16.244' W 80° 57.089'
Private property just outside of the Hockley Valley Nature Reserve

Horning Mills, South Central Region, Dufferin County, Horning
Mills
Plunge Type, Pine River, Rating: 2/4, Access: Moderate
GPS Location: N 44° 09.667' W 80° 11.944'
Off Mill Lane east of Horning Mills

Scotts Falls Lower, South Central Region, Dufferin County, Mono
Center
Curtain Type, Nottawasaga River, Rating: 1/4, Access: Private
GPS Location: N 43° 59.308' W 80° 05.298'
Private

Scotts Falls Upper, South Central Region, Dufferin County, Mono
Center
Curtain Type, Nottawasaga River, Rating: 2/4, Access: Private
GPS Location: N 43° 59.496' W 80° 05.304'
Private

Grey County

Antheas Waterfall, South Central Region, Grey County, Blantyre
Cascade Type, Minniehill Creek, Rating: 1/4, Access: Moderate
GPS Location: N 44° 30.560 W 80° 37.332
East on Bruce Trail NE of Blantyre

Epping Falls, South Central Region, Grey County, Epping
Plunge Type, Unknown Creek, Rating: 1/4, Access: Easy
GPS Location: N 44° 27.456' W 80° 33.046'
Off Sideroad 19 250 m east of ON-17

Eugenia Falls, South Central Region, Grey County, Eugenia Falls
Curtain Type, Beaver River, Rating: 2/4, Access: Easy
GPS Location: N 44° 18.783' W 80° 31.583'
Off Grey Rd. 13 in Eugenia Falls, signed

Fairmount Falls, South Central Region, Grey County, Fairmount
Plunge Type, Unknown River, Rating: 1/4, Access: Private
GPS Location: N 44° 29.670' W 80° 32.730'
Private

Hayward Falls, South Central Region, Grey County, Rocky Saugeen
Overfalls Type, Rocky Saugeen, Rating: 1/4, Access: Private
GPS Location: N 44° 15.005' W 80° 46.981'
Private

Hogg's Falls, South Central Region, Grey County, Flesherton
Curtain Type, Boyne River, Rating: 2/4, Access: Easy
GPS Location: N 44° 17.317' W 80° 32.517'
Off Lower valley Rd. 0.5 km east of E Back Line

Indian Falls

South Central Region
Type: Curtain Type
River and County: Indian Creek, Balmy Beach, Grey County
GPS Location: N 44° 37.267' W 80° 57.25'
Rating: 3/4
Access: Moderate, 15 Minutes
Description:
Although it occasionally suffers from reduced water flows, this is a
great looking falls. It is well worth a visit in the winter too.

Getting There: From Owen Sound, go north on Second Ave. W., off Highway 10, west of Owen Sound. This road becomes Grey Road 1 and continues to Balmy Beach. Park at Indian Falls Conservation area and follow the easy trail to the falls.

Photography Tips: There are excellent set ups spots near the crest. With a bit of work, you can move up to the base by diverting off of the trail just before it begins to rise from the river.

Nearby Attractions: Jones Falls is nearby.

Inglis Falls

South Central Region
Type: Cascade Type
River and County: Sydenham River, Inglis Falls, Grey County
GPS Location: N 44° 31.583' W 80° 56.072'
Rating: 3/4
Access: Easy, 2 Minutes

Description: This is a spectacular falls, and its interesting trails and remnants of an old mill, make it a great place for a family outing. A series of steps across from the falls give excellent viewing opportunities.

Getting There: A few miles south of Owen Sound, take Grey Rd. 18 off of Highway 6. Look for Inglis Falls Rd, on your right. It is well signed.

Photography Tips: This is one of the rare falls that looks better when their is less water in the flow, as it creates an interesting pattern with the rocks. Late summer is a great time.

Nearby Attractions: One of four great waterfalls near Owen Sound. See also Indian and Jones Falls.

Jones Falls

South Central Region
Type: Cascade Type
River and County: Pottawatomi River, Owen Sound, Grey County
GPS Location: N 44° 33.55' W 80° 59.103'
Rating: 3/4
Access: Easy, 2 Minutes

Description: This waterfall is a photographer's delight. It seems to have an amazing amount of small details to set the rushing water against.

Getting There: Jones Falls can be reached by taking Highway 6 out of Owen Sound going north. As you reach the top of the escarpment pull over to the gravel shoulder and look for a trail into the woods. It is only a short walk.

Photography Tips: It is difficult to get this falls in a single frame but there is much to do with details. Look for shots with wildflowers and the old cedars.

Nearby Attractions: Indian, And Inglis Falls are all nearby.

Keefer Falls, South Central Region, Grey County, Annan
Curtain Type, Keefer Creek, Rating: 2/4, Access: Private
GPS Location: N 44° 33.55' W 80° 59.103'
Private

Maxwell Falls, South Central Region, Grey County, Owen Sound
Irregular Cascade Type, Maxwell Creek, Rating: 1/4, Access: Moderate
GPS Location: N 44° 33.300' W 80° 58.854'
Take Bruce Trail south off ON-6 at west end of Owen Sound

McGowan Falls, South Central Region, Grey County, Durham
Cascade Type, Saugeen River, Rating: 2/4, Access: Easy
GPS Location: N 44° 10.733' W 80° 48.567'
Off George St. east of ON-6

Minniehill Falls, South Central Region, Grey County, Heathcote
Cascade Type, Minniehill Creek, Rating: 2/4, Access: Moderate
GPS Location: N 44° 30.666' W 80° 36.039'
In Rocklyn Creek Management Center west of Heathcote

Oxenden Falls, South Central Region, Grey County, Oxenden
Gleason Brook, Rating: 2/4, Access: Private
GPS Location: N 44° 45.545' W 81° 05.268'
Private

Traverston Cascade, South Central Region, Grey County, Flesherton
Cascade Type, Rocky Saugeen River, Rating: 1/4, Access: Private
GPS Location: N 44° 16.170' W 80° 44.694'
Private but viewable from Traverston Rd, between Con. Rd 8 and Grey Road 12

Walters Falls, South Central Region, Walters Falls, Grey County
Plunge Type, Walters Creek, Rating: 2/4, Access: Easy
GPS Location: N 44° 29.333' W 80° 42.7'
End of Front St. in Walters Falls

Weaver Creek Falls (Harrison Park Falls), South Central Region,

Grey County, Owen Sound
Plunge Type, Weaver Creek, Rating: 2/4, Access: Easy
GPS Location: N 44° 32.556' W 80° 56.280'
Take trail near the pool in Harrison Park

Halton County

Hilton Falls, South Central Region, Halton County, Campbellville
Curtain Type, Sixteen Mile Creek, Rating: 2/4, Access: Moderate
GPS Location: N 43° 30.56' W 79° 58.75'
Off Campbellville Rd 4.8 km east of Campbellville

Kilbride Falls, South Central Region, Halton County, Kilbride
Cascade Type, Bronte Creek, Rating: 2/4, Access: Moderate
GPS Location: N 43° 25.141 W 79° 55.863'
About 1 km. south of the town of Kilbride off Cedar Springs Rd.

Limehouse Rapids, South Central Region, Halton County, Limehouse
Rapids Type, Black Creek, Rating: 2/4, Access: Easy
GPS Location: N 43° 38.133' W 79° 58.55'
In Limehouse Conservation Area

Lower Quarry Cascade, South Central Region, Halton County, Burlington
Cascade Type, Surface Creek, Rating: 1/4, Access: Private
GPS Location: N 43° 18.714' W 79° 54.270'
Private

Middle Quarry Cascade, South Central Region, Halton County, Burlington
Cascade Type, Surface Creek, Rating: 1/4, Access: Private
GPS Location: N 43° 18.792' W 79° 54.330'
Private

Silver Creek Falls, South Central Region, Halton County, Glen Williams
Cascade Type, Trib. Snow Creek, Rating: 2/4, Access: Easy
GPS Location: N 43° 41.454' W 79° 58.1756'
In Silver Creek Conservation Area

Snake Falls Lower, South Central Region, Halton County, Burlington
Cascade Type, Trib. Grindstone Creek, Rating: 1/4, Access: Difficult
GPS Location: N 43° 19.567' W 79° 53.267'
Follow the Bruce Trail from Main St in Waterdown for about 20 minutes

Snake Falls Upper, South Central Region, Halton County, Burlington
Cascade Type, Trib. Grindstone Creek, Rating: 2/4, Access: Difficult
GPS Location: N 43° 19.567' W 79° 53.267'
Follow the Bruce Trail from Main St in Waterdown for about 20 minutes

Snow Creek Falls North, South Central Region, Halton County, Silver Creek
Cascade Type, Snow Creek, Rating: 1/4, Access: Easy
GPS Location: N 43° 41.172' W 79° 58.470'
In Silver Creek Conservation Area
Snow Creek Falls West, South Central Region, Halton County, Silver Creek
Cascade Type, Snow Creek, Rating: 2/4, Access: Easy
GPS Location: N 43° 41.454' W 79° 58.175'
In Silver Creek Conservation Area

Huron County

Falls Reserve, South Central Region, Huron County, Goderich
Curtain Type, Maitland River, Rating: 2/4, Access: Easy
GPS Location: N 43° 42.616' W 81° 38.683'
In the Falls Reserve Conservation Area

Lambton County

Ausable River Falls, South Central Region, Lambton County, Arkona
Cascade Type, Ausable River, Rating: 2/4, Access: Private
GPS Location: N 43° 06.384' W 81° 48.546'
Private, Off Elm Tree Dr. NE of Arkona

Rock Glen Falls (Fullers Falls), South Central Region, Lambton County, Arkona
Ribbon Type, Bear Creek, Rating: 2/4, Access: Easy
GPS Location: N 43° 5.1' W 81° 49.233'
In Rock Glen Conservation Area

Peel County

Belfountain Falls, South Central Region, Peel County, Belfountain Town
Plunge-step Type, West Credit River, Rating: 2/4, Access: Easy
GPS Location: N 43° 47.650' W 80° 00.756'
In Belfountain Conservation Area north of Belfountain

Church's Falls Upper (**Cataract Falls Upper**), South Central Region, Peel County, Cataract
Plunge Type, Credit River, Rating: 2/4, Access: Easy
GPS Location: N 43° 49.256' W 80° 1.320'
In Forks of the Credit P.P. south of Cataract

Church's Falls (**Cataract Falls**)

South Central Region
Type: Plunge Type
River and County: Credit River, Cataract, Peel County
GPS Location: N 43° 49.256' W 80° 1.320'
Rating: 3/4
Access: Easy to Difficult, 10 Minute

Description: There is an excellent and easy trail that passes by this falls in the Forks of the Credit Provincial Park. By the side of it is the ruins of an old mill.

Getting There: Just south of the Village of Cataract on Cataract Road, you will find the entrance to Forks of the Credit Provincial Park and the trail to the falls is by the entrance. After crossing the railway tracks, the trail goes over a metal bridge with the Upper Church's Falls below and then curves to the right. After about 200 meters, you will see the main Church's Falls in the gorge below to your right.

Photography Tips: The view from the trail above is both distant and obstructed and some photographers make there way down the slope to get a better view. This slope is loose rock, making the trip difficult and dangerous. There is a line of small trees along the upper edge of the slope which can make the climb easier, but think carefully before risking it.
Nearby Attractions: You pass the Upper Church's Falls on the trail, and Belfountain Falls and Limehouse Rapids are a short drive nearby.

Waterloo County

Devils Creek Falls West, South Central Region, Waterloo County, Cambridge
Cascade Type, Trib. Devils Cr, Rating: 1/4, Access: Easy
GPS Location: N 43° 22.506' W 80° 20.016'
Pull off George St. N 1.9 km north of Park Hill Rd., walk 300m north

Devils Creek Falls, South Central Region, Waterloo County, Cambridge
Cascade Type, Devils Cr, Rating: 2/4, Access: Easy
GPS Location: N 43° 22.506' W 80° 20.016'
Off George St. N 1.9 km north of Park Hill Rd.

Wellington County

Elora Gorge
South Central Region
Type: Cascade Type
River and County: Grand River, Elora, Wellington County
GPS Location: N 43° 40.817' W 80° 25.867'
Rating: 3/4
Access: Easy, 5 Minutes

Description: This is a great place to visit, the whole area around the river is interesting and a great family destination.

Getting There: Elora Gorge can be accessed from the town of Elora. Look for a parking lot by the downtown bridge on Metcalfe St. beside an abandoned furniture factory and you will be beside the best part of it. You can pick up a trail behind the old factory. The rocky island at the crest of the falls has the evocative name "The Tooth of Time".

Photography Tips: If you stay near the river behind the old factory, you will find some ruins of an old millrace where you can cross to a bit of land that comes out across from the mill and the Tooth of Time. Be careful though.
Nearby Attractions: The area is worth a few hours exploring. The river can be accessed from the other side, and there are good places for shoppers. There is also a tube rafting run down the gorge which is fun.

Everton Cascade, South Central Region, Wellington County, Everton Cascade Type, Eramosa River, Rating: 2/4, Access: Easy
GPS Location: N 43° 39.695' W 80° 09.180'
South 300m on Everett St. from Oliphant St. behind Hartop Mill

Fergus Cascade, South Central Region, Wellington County, Fergus Rapids Type, Grand River, Rating: 2/4, Access: Easy
GPS Location: N 43° 42.298' W 80° 22.521'
Off ON-6 in Fergus just west of bridge

Irvine Cascade, South Central Region, Wellington County, Elora
Cascade Type, Irvine Creek, Rating: 2/4, Access: Easy
GPS Location: N 43° 41.6' W 80° 26.683'
Off bridge on Woolwich St. W. north of Wellington Rd. 7

Little Elora Waterfall, South Central Region, Wellington County,
Elora
Cascade Type, Trib. Grand River, Rating: 2/4, Access: Moderate
GPS Location: N 43° 40.231' W 80° 27.021'
Viewable from Elora Gorge Conservation area

Rockwood Falls, South Central Region, Wellington County,
Rockwood

Cascade Type, Eramosa River, Rating: 2/4, Access: Moderate
GPS Location: N 43°36.755' W 80° 08.867'
In Rockwood Conservation Area

Cottage Country Region

Haliburton County

Brandy Falls, Cottage Country Region, Haliburton County, Dorset
cascade Type, Ernest Lake, Rating: 1/4, Access: Difficult
GPS Location: N 45° 13.068' W 78° 48.906'
Canoe or extended hike. Often dry

Buttermilk Falls (Haliburton), Cottage Country Region, Haliburton
County, Buttermilk Falls
Slide Type, Kennisis River, Rating: 2/4, Access: Easy
GPS Location: N 45° 5.719' W 78° 44.783'
Off Highway 35 in the town of Buttermilk Falls

Castor Oil Chute, Cottage Country Region, Haliburton County,
Kennaway
Chute Type, York River, Rating: 1/4, Access: Easy
GPS Location: N 45° 15.007' W 78° 14.972'
Located in the south of Algonquin P.P.

Cope Falls, Cottage Country Region, Haliburton County, Gooderham
Overfalls Type, Wilberemere Lake, Rating: 1/4, Access: Easy
GPS Location: N 44° 59.005' W 78° 12.974'
By ON-118 NE of Gooderham

Drag River Falls, Cottage Country Region, County, Gelert
Cascade Type, Drag River, Rating: 2/4, Access: Difficult
GPS Location: N 44° 53.868' W 78° 37.098'
In Gelert, 300 m west of Francis Rd.

Elliott Falls
Cottage Country Region
Type: Cascade Type
River and County: Gull River, Norland, Haliburton County
GPS Location: N 44° 44.583' W 78° 49.483'
Rating: 3/4
Access: Easy, 10 Minutes

Description: This area offers a pleasant walkway around the area of the falls and a natural setting.
Getting There: Take Highway 35 north from Norland for about 2.5 km. and make a right on Elliott Falls Road. Go to the end of the road.

Photography Tips: There are a lot of shrubs along the river's edge, so you will need to take some time to find open views.
Nearby Attractions: It is about 1/2 hour drive to Rackety Falls

Furnace Falls, Cottage Country Region, Haliburton County, Furnace Falls
Curtain Type, Irondale River, Rating: 2/4, Access: Easy
GPS Location: N 44° 49.567' W 78° 33.733'
Off County Rd 503 about 1.2 km north of White Boundary Rd.

Gooderham Falls, Cottage Country Region, Haliburton County, Gooderham
Cascade Type, Irondale River, Rating: 2/4, Access: Easy
GPS Location: N 44° 54.467' W 78° 22.867'
Off Lakeshore Rd north of ON-503 in Gooderham

Gut Rapids, Cottage Country Region, Haliburton County, Algonquin P.P.
Rapids Type, York River, Rating: 1/4, Access: Moderate
GPS Location: N 45° 13.182' W 78° 10.284'
In Algonquin P.P. at south end of Byers Lake, canoe.

High Falls (York River), Cottage Country Region, Haliburton County, Kennaway
Cascade Type, York River, Rating: 2/4, Access: Difficult
GPS Location: N 45° 12.409' W 7u8° 09.369'
Canoe or extended hike

Kennisis Falls, Cottage Country Region, Haliburton County, Carnarvon
Chute Type, Big Hawk Lake, Rating: 1/4, Access: Easy
GPS Location: N 45° 8.541' W 78° 44.589'
By Big Hawk Lake Rd. north of Carnarvon

Kinmount Cascade, Cottage Country Region, Haliburton County, Kinmount
Rapid Type, Burnt River, Rating: 1/4, Access: Easy
GPS Location: N 44° 46.830' W 78° 39.144'
In the town of Kinmount, a dam at the top.

Long Slide

Cottage Country Region
Type: Cascade Type
River and County: Hollow River, Dorset, Haliburton County
GPS Location: N 45° 15.391' W 78° 51.502'
Rating: 3/4
Access: Easy trail difficulty, 2 Minutes

Description: The water rushes through the narrows of the Hollow
River with great force. It is a spectacular setting in the fall.
Getting There: Take County Rd 8 east from Hwy 35 north of Dorset
and you will reach a small park in about 2.3 km.
Photography Tips: The foreground rock ledges are a good complement
to the water and trees.

Minden Whitewater Preserve, Cottage Country Region, Haliburton
County, Carnavon
Cascade-Rapids Type, Gull River, Rating: 2/4, Access: Moderate
GPS Location: N 44° 58.062' W 78° 40.998'
On Duck Lake Rd south of Carnavon

Moore Falls, Cottage Country Region, Haliburton County, Moore
Falls
Obliterated by dam, Black Lake, Rating: 1/4
GPS Location: N 44° 48.337' W 78° 48.171'
Off Hwy ON-35 in Moore Falls

Nunikani Dam Falls, Cottage Country Region, Haliburton County,
Little Hawk Lake
Cascade Type, Nunikani Lake, Rating: 2/4, Access: Moderate
GPS Location: N 45° 11.072' W 78° 44.688'
Canoe

Rackety Falls, Cottage Country Region, Haliburton County, Minden
Cascade Type, Bob Creek, Rating: 2/4, Access: Moderate
GPS Location: N 44° 51.967' W 78° 46.706'
Found on Rackety Trail south of Minden

Ragged Falls
Cottage Country Region
Type: Cascade Type

River and County: Oxtongue River, Dwight, Haliburton County
GPS Location: N 45° 23.450' W 78° 54.348'
Rating: 3/4
Access: Moderate trail difficulty, 15 Minutes

Description: An impressive extended cascade falls found in Ragged
Falls Provincial Park, just west of Algonquin Provincial Park
Getting There: From Huntsville take ON-60 east towards Algonquin
Provincial Park and after 32 km you will see the turn into Ragged Falls
Provincial Park
Photography Tips: There is a trail along the east side of the falls which
offers a great many photo opportunities.

Ritchie Falls (Lower, Middle and Upper)
Cottage Country Region
Type: Cascade Type
River and County: Burnt Creek, Lochlin, Haliburton County
GPS Location: N 44° 55.699' W 78° 35.675'
Rating: 3/4
Access: Easy trail difficulty, 5 Minutes

Description: This series of three falls is easy to access and great to photograph.

Getting There: From the town of Lochlin go west on Gelert Rd and after 250 m. turn left on Ritchie Rd. The falls are 2.6 km. along the road.

Photography Tips: There is a trail along the river which offers multiple opportunities for great images.

The Buckslides, Cottage Country Region, Haliburton County, Peterson Corner
Rapids Type, Boshkung River, Rating: 2/4, Access: Moderate
GPS Location: N 45° 03.272' W 78° 45.093'
Off Buckslides Rd north of Peterson Corner

Three Brothers Falls, Cottage Country Region, Haliburton County, Kinmount
Cascade Type, Burnt River, Rating: 3/4, Access: Difficult
GPS Location: N 44° 51.936' W 78° 36.719'
Private land, perhaps legal access by canoe'

Tim River Falls, Muskoka Region, Haliburton County, Algonquin P.P.
Rapids Type, Tim River, Rating: 1/4, Access: Moderate
GPS Location: N 45° 44.032' W 78° 52.239'
Canoe

Tim Road Cascades, Muskoka Region, Haliburton County, Strong
Cascades Type, Tim River, Rating: 1/4, Access: Moderate
GPS Location: N 45° 40.532' W 79° 07.566'
Off Forestry Road

Witney Rapids, Cottage Region, Haliburton County, Whitney
Rapids Type, Madawaska River, Rating: 1/4, Access: Easy
GPS Location: N 45° 29.658' W 78° 14.355'
Off ON-60

The Kawarthas

Big Eddy, Cottage Country Region, Kawartha County, Severn Bridge
Cascade Type, Black River, Rating: 2/4, Access: Moderate
GPS Location: N 44° 47.708' W 79° 12.273'
Off intersection Regional Rd 6 and Black River Rd

Fenelon Falls, Cottage Country Region, Kawartha County, Fenelon
Falls
Curtain Type, Cameron Lake, Rating: 1/4, Access: Easy
GPS Location: N 44° 32.161' W 78° 44.243'
Found in the center of the town of the same name

Ragged Rapids, Cottage Country Region, Kawartha County, Bala
Waterfall Type, Black River, Rating: 1/4, Access: Moderate
GPS Location: N 45° 01.057' W 79°41.255'
Obliterated by dam.

Victoria Falls, Cottage Country Region, Kawartha County, Riley Lake
Cascade Type, Black River, Rating: 2/4, Access: Moderate
GPS Location: N 44° 49.988' W 79° 03.574'
Off Black River Rd and Montgomery Rd

Muskoka County

Bala Falls (Upper and Lower), Cottage Country Region, Muskoka
County, Bala
Cascade Type, Moon River, Rating: 2/4, Access: Easy
GPS Location: N 45° 00.729' W 79° 36.882'
Off Bala Falls Road.

Baysville Dam, Cottage Country Region, Muskoka County, Baysville
Dam, Muskoka River, Rating: 1/4, Access: Easy
GPS Location: N 45° 09.173' W 79° 06.778'
Obliterated by dam

Big Chute, Cottage Country Region, Muskoka County, Big Chute
Cascade Type, Severn River, Rating: 2/4, Access: Easy
GPS Location: N 44° 53.141' W 79° 40.588'
Off County Rd 34 in Big Chute

Big Eddy Rapids, Cottage Country Region, Muskoka County, Bala
Rapids Type, Musquash River, Rating: 1/4, Access: Moderate
GPS Location: N 45° 01.252' W 79° 45.145'
At the end of unnamed rd off Iroquois Cranberry Marsh Rd.

Bracebridge Falls Lower

Cottage Country Region
Type: Cascade Type
River and County: Muskoka River, Bracebridge, Muskoka County
GPS Location: N 45° 2.317' W 79° 18.483'
Rating: 3/4
Access: Easy, 2 Minutes

Description: Although it is in an urban area and surrounded by man made objects, the shear volume of this falls makes it interesting.
Getting There: You can take Highway 16 into the center of the town and park near the bridge.
Photography Tips: Take the park walkway beside the river and you will find multiple spots for open views.
Nearby Attractions: Bracebridge Falls upper is a short walk and Wilson's and High Falls are a short drive.

Bracebridge Falls Upper

Cottage Country Region
Type: Cascade Type
River and County: Muskoka River, Bracebridge, Muskoka County
GPS Location: N 45° 2.317' W 79° 18.483'
Rating: 3/4

Access: Easy, 2 Minutes

Description: Found in an urban area and surrounded by man made objects, it is still an interesting falls.
Getting There: You can take Highway 16 into the center of the town and park near the bridge.
Photography Tips: Take the park walkway beside the river and you will find multiple spots for open views.
Nearby Attractions: Bracebridge Falls lower is a short walk and Wilson's and High Falls are a short drive.

Bullhead Falls, Cottage Country Region, Muskoka County, Bracebridge
Cascade Type, Spence Lake inlet, Rating: 1/4, Access: Difficult
GPS Location: N 45° 00.358' W 79° 14.629'
Canoe or extended hike

Clark Falls, Cottage Country Region, Muskoka County, Dee Bank
Cascade Type, Dee River, Rating: 2/4, Access: Moderate
GPS Location: N 45° 10.603' W 79° 33.362'
Hike but probably private property

Crozier Falls, Cottage Country Region, Muskoka County, Fraserburg
Cascade Type, Muskoka River, Rating: 2/4, Access: Moderate
GPS Location: N 45° 02.351' W 79° 07.669'
Off south end Sherwood Forest Rd.

Curtain Chute, Cottage Country Region, Muskoka County, MacTier
Rapids Type, Moon River, Rating: 1/4, Access: Difficult
GPS Location: N 45° 05.123' W 79° 51.222'
Canoe or extended hike

Dee Bank Falls
Cottage Country Region
Type: Cascade Type
River and County: Dee River, Dee Banks, Muskoka County
GPS Location: N 45° 10.79' W 79° 31.179'
Rating: 3/4
Access: Easy Trail difficulty, Minute

Description:
A quiet natural setting you will likely have to yourself. The smooth rocks are interesting.
Getting There: From Highway 141 at Ulswater go south on Highway 24 for about 5 km. There are areas to park by the side of the road at the bridge.
Photography Tips: You can move along the north bank and find some great places to set up.
Nearby Attractions: Hatchery and Minnehaha Falls are a short drive.

Distress Chute, Cottage Country Region, Muskoka County, Big East River P.P.
Cascade Type, Big East River, Rating: 2/4, Access: Moderate
GPS Location: N 45° 27.818' W 79° 05.133'
Canoe, In Big East River P.P.

Duck Chutes, Cottage Country Region, Muskoka County, Bracebridge
Rapids Type, Muskoka River, Rating: 1/4, Access: Moderate
GPS Location: N 45° 07.155' W 79° 18.198'
Off the north end of Alpine Ranch Rd.

Fairy Falls, Cottage Country Region, Muskoka County, Baysville
Cascade Type, Muskoka River, Rating: 2/4, Access: Moderate
GPS Location: N 45° 06.833' W 79° 07.066'
Off Fairy Falls Rd. south of Baysville

Flat Rapids, Cottage Country Region, Muskoka County, MacTier
Rapids Type, Go Home River, Rating: 1/4, Access: Moderate
GPS Location: N 45° 02.040' W 79° 09.008'
Canoe or extended hike

Flat Rock Rapids, Cottage Country Region, Muskoka County,
MacTier
Rapids Type, Go Home River, Rating: 1/4, Access: Moderate
GPS Location: N 45° 01.937' W 79° 51.285'
Canoe or extended hike

Go Home Chute, Cottage Country Region, Muskoka County,
MacTier
Chute Type, Go Home River, Rating: 1/4, Access: Moderate
GPS Location: N 45° 00.908' W 79° 53.177'
Canoe or extended hike

Gravel Falls, Cottage Country Region, Muskoka County, Dwight
Plunge Type, Oxtongue River, Rating: 3/4, Access: Moderate
GPS Location: N 45° 24.673' W 78° 53.899'
Off Timbertrail Ln north of ON-60

Hanna Chute, Cottage Country Region, Muskoka County,
Bracebridge
Dam, Muskoka River, Rating: 1/4, Access: Easy
GPS Location: N 45° 00.049' W 79° 17.869'
Obliterated by dam

Hardy Lake Falls, Cottage Country Region, Muskoka County, Hardy
Lake P.P.
Waterfall Type, Hardy Lake outlet, Rating: 1/4, Access: Easy
GPS Location: N 45° 00.744' W 79° 31.472'
Found by Hardy Lake Trail

Hatchery Falls
Cottage Country Region
Type: Cascade Type

River and County: Skeleton River, Rousseau, Muskoka County
GPS Location: N 45° 13.367' W 79° 30.967'
Rating: 3/4
Access: Moderate trail difficulty, 20 Minutes

Description: A short walk from the parking area brings you to this lovely falls
Getting There: Found off Fish Hatchery Rd, north of ON-141
Photography Tips: A trail alongside the falls takes you to various interesting vantage points.

High Falls (Bracebridge)
Cottage Country Region
Type: Cascade Type
River and County: Muskoka River, Bracebridge, Muskoka County
GPS Location: N 45° 5.286' W 79° 18.090'
Rating: 3/4
Access: Easy trail difficulty, 2 Minutes

Description: A fabulous falls found close to ON-11. Great spot for a family visit.

Getting There: Getting There: In Bracebridge take Cedar Lane west off ON-11 and in a short distance take the first right and follow it to the end. Don't take High Falls Rd.
Photography Tips: There are multiple spots to set up along the side of the falls.
Nearby Attractions: Little High Falls and Potts Falls

Hogs Trough, Cottage Country Region, Muskoka County, Dwight
Cascade Type, Oxtongue River, Rating: 2/4, Access: Easy
GPS Location: N 45° 20.228' W 78° 56.689'
Off Oxtongue Rapids Park Road

Hood Rapids, Cottage Country Region, Muskoka County, Etwell
Rapids Type, Buck River, Rating: 2/4, Access: Easy
GPS Location: N 45° 21.860' W 79° 20.651'
Off Hoodstown Rd northeast of Etwell

Island Portage Falls, Cottage Country Region, Muskoka County, Bala
Cascade Type, Moon River, Rating: 2/4, Access: Moderate
GPS Location: N 45° 01.950' W 79° 42.990'
Canoe or extended hike

Kashe River Cascade, Cottage Country Region, Muskoka County, Kashe Lake
Cascade Type, Kashe River, Rating: 1/4, Access: Moderate
GPS Location: N 44° 50.188' W 79° 18.862'
Off ON-11 in Kashe Lake

Little High Falls, Cottage Country Region, Muskoka County, Bracebridge
Cascade Type, Potts Creek, Rating: 2/4, Access: Easy
GPS Location: N 45° 5.333' W 79° 18.083'
Off High Falls Rd from ON-11

Marsh Falls, Cottage Country Region, Muskoka County, Dwight
Cascade Type, Oxtongue River, Rating: 2/4
GPS Location: N 45° 18.750' W 78° 59.348'
Private property

Matthiasville Falls, Cottage Country Region, Muskoka County, Matthiasville
Dam, Muskoka River, Rating: 1/4, Access: Easy
GPS Location: N 44° 59.662' W 79° 12.125'
Obliterated by a dam

May Chutes, Cottage Country Region, Muskoka County, Fraserburg
Chute Type, Muskoka River, Rating: 1/4, Access: Moderate
GPS Location: N 45° 03.272' W 79° 07.706'
Off Sherwood Forest Dr. south of Fraserburg

McCutcheons Falls, Cottage Country Region, Muskoka County, Vankoughnet
Cascade Type, Black River, Rating: 3/4, Access: Easy
GPS Location: N 44° 59.526' W 79° 02.944'
Off Vankoughnet Rd north of Vankoughnet

McDonald River Falls, Cottage Country Region, Muskoka County, Honey Harbour
Cascade Type, McDonald River, Rating: 1/4, Access: Moderate
GPS Location: N 44° 55.672' W 79° 46.989'
Canoe or extended hike

Minnehaha Falls(Muskoka)

Cottage Country Region
Type: Cascade Type
River and County: Skeleton River, Ullswater, Muskoka County
GPS Location: N 45° 13.239' W 79° 31.388'
Rating: 3/4
Access: Difficult trail difficulty, 10 Minutes

Description: A beautiful wild falls but probably overlooked because of
the difficult access.
Getting There: Go 2.5 km west of Ullswater on ON-141 and the falls is
down the hill to the right. The slope is very steep. If you go to the east
end, you will find a rock filled drainage channel topped by a steel
culvert. This is the easiest descent.
Photography Tips: There are good setup spots near the crest and the
base.

Moon Falls, Cottage Country Region, Muskoka County, MacTier
Cascade Type, Moon River, Rating: 3/4, Access: Difficult
GPS Location: N 45° 06.181' W 79° 55.375'
Canoe

Muskoka Falls

Cottage Country Region
Type: Cascade-Chute Type
River and County: Muskoka River, Bracebridge, Muskoka County
GPS Location: N 44° 59.514' W 79° 17.867'
Rating: 3/4
Access: Moderate trail difficulty, 5 Minutes

Description: Although it is surrounded by man made elements, the sheer power of this falls makes it a spectacle.
Getting There: From ON-11 take exit 184 and follow Cedar Lane/ Frederick St Rd then keep left at the fork and follow the signs for Muskoka Falls
Photography Tips: There are multiple places to shoot from but you need to position carefully if you want to exclude man made elements

Mye River Cascades, Cottage Country Region, Muskoka County
Cascade Type, Mye River, Rating: 1/4, Access: Moderate
GPS Location: N 44° 53.392' W 79° 41.733'
Off White Falls Rd

Ox Tongue Rapids

Cottage Country Region
Type: Rapids Type
River and County: Oxtongue River, Dwight, Muskoka County
GPS Location: N 45° 20.055' W 78° 56.817'
Rating: 4/4
Access: Easy trail difficulty, 1 Minute

Description: Although it is only a rapids, I have given it a high rating because it one of the most beautiful locations I have seen, especially so when the fall foliage is at its peak.
Getting There: Take Oxtongue Rapids Rd off ON-60 about 3.2 km east of Dwight and you will see excellent areas as the road parallels the river.
Photography Tips: fall is certainly the preferred time to visit. You can stop at any of the pull offs and walk along the river.

Peterson Falls, Cottage Country Region, Muskoka County, Vankoughnet
Cascade Type, Black River, Rating: 2/4, Access: Moderate
GPS Location: N 44° 58.479' W 79° 02.940'
Off Old Victoria Rd. south of Vankoughnet

Port Sydney Falls

Cottage Country Region
Type: Slide Type
River and County: Muskoka River, Port Sydney, Muskoka County
GPS Location: N 45° 12.933' W 79° 16.533'
Rating: 3/4
Access: Easy trail difficulty, 1 Minute

Description: Colorful bedrock ledges contain this long gentle falls, a great place to visit.
Getting There: Take exit 207 from ON-11 and follow Regional Road 10 toward Port Sydney. In 4.2 miles after driving along the lake you will reach a parking area and the falls.
Photography Tips: You can walk along the rock ledges and get great shots with the trees is the far ground.

Potts Falls, Cottage Country Region, Muskoka County, Bracebridge
Waterfall Type, Potts Creek, Rating: 2/4, Access: Easy
GPS Location: N 45° 5.333' W 79° 18.083'
Off High Falls Rd from ON-11

Pretty Channel Rapids, Cottage Country Region, Muskoka County,
Big Chute
Rapids Type, Severn River, Rating: 1/4, Access: Easy
GPS Location: N 44° 53.069' W 79° 40.429'
Off Upper Big Chute Rd in Big Chute

Rosseau Falls (Lower)

Cottage Country Region
Type: Cascade Type
River and County: Rosseau River, Rosseau, Muskoka County
GPS Location: N 45° 13.928' W 79° 35.719'
Rating: 3/4
Access: Easy trail difficulty, 2 Minutes

Description: A beautiful falls found in a quiet natural setting
Getting There: Found on Rosseau Lake Rd 3 2.4 km south of ON-141
Photography Tips: There are colorful rock ledges which allow multiple
setup spots
Nearby Attractions: Rosseau Falls (Upper)

Rosseau Falls (Upper), Cottage Country Region, Muskoka County, Rosseau
Cascade Type, Rosseau River, Rating: 2/4, Access: Easy
GPS Location: N 45° 14.375' W 79° 35.076'
Found on ON-141 6 km east of Rosseau

Sandy **Gray Rapids,** Cottage Country Region, Muskoka County, Town
Rapids Type, Musquash River, Rating: 1/4, Access: Moderate
GPS Location: N 45° 02.032' W 79° 49.051'
Canoe

Slater Falls, Cottage Country Region, Muskoka County, Baysville
Cascade Type, Muskoka River, Rating: 1/4, Access: Moderate
GPS Location: N 45° 05.116' W 79° 09.063'
Off Colony Rd south of Baysville

Stubbs Falls

Cottage Country Region
Type: Cascade Type
River and County: Little East River, Huntsville, Muskoka County
GPS Location: N 45° 22.944' W 79° 12.445'
Rating: 3/4
Access: Easy trail difficulty, 10 Minutes

Description: The Little East River runs down through a hollow of colorful rock in this wild natural setting.
Getting There: From the town of Huntsville go north on Muskoka Rd 3 for 3.7 km and enter Arrowhead Provincial Park where you will find the falls.
Photography Tips: From the bridge, it is easy to move down along the river edge and set up along the rocks.

Tea Falls, Muskoka Region, Haliburton County, Dwight
Cascade Type, Oxtongue River, Rating: 2/4, Access: Easy
GPS Location: N 45°29.448' W 78° 45.060'
Off ON-60 in Algonquin Park

Three Rock Chute, Cottage Country Region, Muskoka County, MacTier
Chute Type, Musquash River, Rating: 1/4, Access: Difficult
GPS Location: N 44° 58.56' W 79° 51.159'
Canoe only

Trethewey Falls, Cottage Country Region, Muskoka County, Muskoka Falls
Dam, Muskoka River, Rating: 1/4, Access: Easy
GPS Location: N 44° 59.304' W 79° 16.288'
Obliterated

Twin Falls Upper, Cottage Country Region, Haliburton County, Algonquin P.P.
Cascade Type, Oxtongue River, Rating: 2/4, Access: Moderate
GPS Location: N 45° 40.529' W 78° 47.118'
Canoe

Whites Falls, Cottage Country Region, Muskoka County, Big Chute
Cascade Type, Six Mile Lake, Rating: 1/4, Access: Easy
GPS Location: N 44° 52.830' W 79° 43.340'
Dam at crest, On-34 2.4 km east of Hwy 400

Wilsons Falls
Cottage Country Region
Type: Cascade Type

River and County: North Branch Muskoka River , Bracebridge,
Muskoka County
GPS Location: N 45° 3.567' W 79° 18.467'
Rating: 3/4
Access: Easy trail difficulty, 10 Minutes

Description: One of the finest of the Bracebridge areas many
waterfalls. While there is a dam her it is very unobtrusive. There is an
excellent trail which offers good views.
Getting There: From ON-37 Manitoba St. go west on Taylor Rd and
turn left on River Rd, continuing on Wilsons Falls Rd to the end. There
is a parking lot there.
Photography Tips: Move along the trail and move to the shore when
you see likely spots. In fall you will find excellent foliage for both the
foreground and background.
Nearby Attractions: Bracebridge Falls, High Falls (Bracebridge) and
Muskoka Falls

Simcoe County

Cooper's Falls, Cottage Country Region, Simcoe County, Cooper's
Falls
Cascade Type, Black River, Rating: 2/4, Access: Private
GPS Location: N 44° 47.336' W 79° 13.852'
Private but viewable from ON-11

Lavender Falls, Cottage Country Region, Simcoe County,
Collingwood
Cascade Type, Noisy River, Rating: 2/4, Access: Private
GPS Location: N 44° 15.906' W 80° 12.496'
Private Property

Little Falls, Cottage Country Region, Simcoe County, Washago
Dam, Rating: 1/4, Access: Easy
GPS Location: N 44° 44.786' W 79° 19.504'
Obliterated by dam

Port Severn Rapids, Cottage Country Region, Simcoe County, Port
Severn
Dam, Outlet to Georgian Bay, Rating: 1/4, Access: Easy
GPS Location: N 44° 48.216' W 79° 43.326'
Obliterated by dam

Wasdell Rapids, Cottage Country Region, Simcoe County, Severn
Bridge
Rapids Type, Severn River, Rating: 1/4, Access: Easy
GPS Location: N 44° 46.872' W 79° 17.632'
Off Laidlaw Ave east off Severn Bridge

Eastern Region

Frontenac County

Bedford Mills Falls, Eastern Region, Frontenac County, Town

Cascade Type, Devil Lake, Rating: 2/4, Access: Easy
GPS Location: N 44° 36.241' W 76° 24.346'
Pull off Perth Road north of Massassauga Rd.

Belleville Rapids, Eastern Region, Frontenac County, Belleville
Rapids Type, Moira River, Rating: 1/4, Access: Easy
GPS Location: N 44° 11.190' W 76° 23.076'
Cannifton Rd in Belleville parallels the rapids.

Birch Rapids, Eastern Region, Frontenac County, Ompah
Rapids Type, Mississippi River, Rating: 1/4, Access: Moderate
GPS Location: N 44° 58.008' W 76° 49.962'
Canoe

Black Rapids, Eastern Region, Frontenac County, Lyndhurst
Rapids Type, Rideau Canal, Rating: 1/4, Access: Easy
GPS Location: N 44° 30.570' W 76° 05.526'
Obliterated by a Lock on the Rideau Canal

Kings Chute, Eastern Region, Frontenac County, Perth
Cascade Type, Mississippi River, Rating: 1/4, Access: Moderate
GPS Location: N 44° 56.094' W 76° 45.120'
Canoe or hike

Kings Falls, Eastern Region, Frontenac County, Perth
Cascade Type, Mississippi River, Rating: 1/4, Access: Moderate
GPS Location: N 44° 56.306' W 76° 46.418'
From the south end of Morrow Rd off Road 509 west of Perth

Kingston Mills Falls, Eastern Region, Frontenac County, Kingston
Cascade Type, Cataraqui River, Rating: 2/4, Access: Easy
GPS Location: N 44° 17.604' W 76° 26.418'
Just east of Kingston Mills Lock north of Kingston

Ragged Chute, Eastern Region, Frontenac County, Perth
Rapids Type, Mississippi River, Rating: 2/4, Access: Moderate
GPS Location: N 44° 56.628' W 76° 43.472'
A short hike from south end of Ragged Chute Rd off Rd 509 west of
Perth

Whitefish Rapids, Eastern Region, Frontenac County, Myers Cave
Rapids Type, Mississippi River, Rating: 1/4, Access: Easy
GPS Location: N 44° 50.515' W 77° 06.901'
South on Whitefish Rapids Ln 3/4 km from Road 506

Hastings County

Big Chute, Eastern Region, Hastings County, Bancroft
Chute Type, Little Mississippi River, Rating: 2/4, Access: Moderate
GPS Location: N 45° 06.5160' W 77° 32.051'
Off Mayo Lake Rd. 30 km east of Bancroft

Callaghan Rapids, Eastern Region, Hastings County, Marmora
Cascade Type, Crowe River, Rating: 1/4, Access: Easy
GPS Location: N 44° 26.482' W 77° 41.393'
Off the end of Callaghan Rapids Road SW Marmora

Chisholm Mills Falls, Eastern Region, Hastings County, Chisholm Mills
Plunge Type, Moira River, Rating: 2/4, Access: Easy
GPS Location: N 44° 21.205' W 77° 18.475'
In Chisholm Mills at the bridge on Shannonville Rd.

Cordova Falls

Eastern Region
Type: Cascade Type
River and County: Crowe River , Cordova Mines, Peterborough County
GPS Location: N 44° 33.367' W 77° 49.497'
Rating: 3/4
Access: Moderate trail difficulty, 15 Minutes

Description: The falls is extended in three sections with a dam at the top.
Getting There: From the village of Cordova Mines head west on County Road 48 and after 1.7 km take the 2nd right onto Preston Rd and then in 0.8 km. take the 1st right onto Fire Route 18. The entrance to the falls area is in 2.7 km

Photography Tips: You can walk along the edge of the falls and get multiple points to set up.

Egan Chute, Eastern Region, Hastings County, Bancroft
Cascade Type, York River, Rating: 2/4, Access: Easy
GPS Location: N 45° 04.656' W 77° 44.253'
In Egan Chute P.P. north of Bancroft on ON-28

Farm Chute, Eastern Region, Hastings County, Egan Chutes P.P.
Cascade Type, York River, Rating: 2/4, Access: Moderate
GPS Location: N 45° 04.996' W 77° 44.868'
Canoe or extended hike

High Falls (**Actinolite**), Eastern Region, Hastings County, Madoc
Cascade Type, Skootamatta River, Rating: 2/4, Access: Moderate
GPS Location: N 44° 33.879' W 77° 19.599'
End of Forbes Rd off County-25 and walk west 800 m.

High Falls (**Papineau Creek**), Eastern Region, Hastings County, Maple Leaf
Cascade Type, Papineau Creek, Rating: 2/4, Access: Difficult
GPS Location: N 45 17' W 77° 49.333'
Off ON-62 2.2 km NE of Musclow Greenview Rd.

High Falls (**York River**), Eastern Region, Hastings County, Bird's Creek
Cascade Type, York River, Rating: 2/4, Access: Easy
GPS Location: N 45° 6.967' W 77° 54.983'
Off Ray Rd north of Bancroft

Jelly Rapids, Eastern Region, Hastings County, Glanmire
Rapids Type, Glanmire Lake, Rating: 2/4, Access: Easy
GPS Location: N 44° 45.150' W 77° 40.896'
Off Old Hastings Rd at north end Glanmire

McArthur Falls, Eastern Region, Hastings County, McArthur Falls
Cascade Type, Little Mississippi River, Rating: 2/4, Access: Easy
GPS Location: N 45° 7.6' W 77° 34.3'
Off ON-28 in McArthur Falls

Middle Chute, Eastern Region, Hastings County, Bancroft
Chute Type, York River, Rating: 2/4, Access: Moderate
GPS Location: N 45° 04.997' W 77° 44.865'
In Egan Chutes P.P. east of Bancroft

Nueman Falls, Eastern Region, Hastings County, Maple Leaf
Cascade Type, Papineau Creek, Rating: 2/4, Access: Moderate
GPS Location: N 45° 15.5' W 77° 52.15'
Off Franzr Rd west of Maple Leaf

Price Rapids, Eastern Region, Hastings County, Madoc
Rapids Type, Skootamatta River, Rating: 2/4, Access: Easy
GPS Location: N 44° 32.867' W 77° 19.656'
Off ON-7 just west of ON-37

Robinson Falls, Eastern Region, Hastings County, Maynooth
Cascade Type, Mink Lake, Rating: 2/4, Access: Moderate
GPS Location: N 45° 17.127' W 78° 05.586'
North of Minke Lake Rd. NW of Maynooth

The Gut

Eastern Ontario Region
Type: Cascade Type
River and County: Crowe River, Lake, Hastings County
GPS Location: N 44° 46.024' W 77° 52.6'
Rating: 3/4
Access: Moderate, 10 Minutes

Description: Located in the Crowe River Conservation Area, the falls are formed when the Crowe River takes a sharp turn into a narrow canyon. Excellent spot for a family outing.
Getting There: From the intersection of Highway 46 and Highway 504, take Hwy 504 (Lasswade Rd.) east for 8.3 km., and make a right on the Gut Trail. Follow it to the parking lot and take the trail down to the falls.
Photography Tips: There are some interesting rocks you can use in the foreground. Look also for panoramas.
Nearby Attractions: The Crowe Conservation Area where the falls is located is a nice natural place to visit.

Triplebee Falls, Eastern Region, Hastings County, Madoc
Waterfall Type, Black River, Rating: 2/4, Access: Moderate
GPS Location: N 44° 39.189' W 77° 26.706'
Off Lingham Lake Rd. NE of Madoc

Lanark County

Appleton Rapids, Eastern Region, Lanark County, Appleton
Rapids Type, Mississippi River, Rating: 1/4, Access: Easy
GPS Location: N 45° 10.982' W 76° 07.491'
Off River Road west of County 17 in Appleton

Arklan Rapids, Eastern Region, Lanark County, Carleton Place
Rapids Type, Mississippi River, Rating: 1/4, Access: Easy
GPS Location: N 45° 8.616' W 76° 08.568'
View from the Rosamund St Bridge in Carleton Place

Blakeney Rapids, Eastern Region, Lanark County, Blackney
Rapids Type, Mississippi River, Rating: 1/4, Access: Easy
GPS Location: N 45° 16.012' W 76° 14.953'
Off Blackney Rd in Blackney

Carleton Place Cascade, Eastern Region, Lanark County, Carleton Place
Dam, Mississippi River, Rating: 1/4, Access: Easy
GPS Location: N 45° 08.483' W 76° 08.747'
Replaced by a dam

Chaffey Lock Cascade, Eastern Region, Lanark County, Chaffey Lock
Rapids Type, Rideau River, Rating: 2/4, Access: Easy
GPS Location: N 44° 34.755' W 76° 19.249'
NW on ON-15 and left on Chaffey's Lock Road

Grand Falls (Almonte)

Eastern Region
Type: Step Cascade Type
River and County: Mississippi River, Almonte, Lanark County
GPS Location: N 45° 13.517' W 76° 11.852'
Rating: 3/4
Access: Easy trail difficulty, 1 Minute

Description: Found in the heart of Almonte, it powered the Victoria Woolen Mill, one of the early industries in the region.
Getting There: The Victoria Woolen Mill building is at the intersection of Main and Mill St in Almonte and the waterfall is behind the building
Photography Tips: You will need a wide lens.

Mill Falls (Almonte), Eastern Region, Lanark County, Almonte
Cascade Type, Mississippi River, Rating: 2/4, Access: Easy
GPS Location: N 45° 13.648' W 76° 11.991'
Found at north end of Mary St. in Almonte

Mill of Kintail Rapids, Eastern Region, Lanark Cty, Bennies Corners
Rapids Type, Indian River, Rating: 1/4, Access: Easy
GPS Location: N 45° 14.684' W 76° 15.474'
1 km SE of Bennies Corners on Ramsay Concession 8

Old Sly Lockes Cascade, Eastern Region, Lanark County, Smiths
Falls
Rapids Type, Rideau Canal, Rating: 1/4, Access: Easy
GPS Location: N 44° 53.491' W 76° 00.333'
By Old Slys Rd in Smiths Falls

Smiths Falls, Eastern Region, Lanark County, Smiths Falls
Dam, Rideau Canal, Rating: 1/4, Access: Easy
GPS Location: N 44° 53.832' W 76° 01.302'
In Smiths Fall found by Rideau Canal Museum, Confederation Dr.

Tays Rapids, Eastern Region, Lanark County, Perth
Rapids Type, Tay River, Rating: 1/4, Access: Easy
GPS Location: N 44° 53.933' W 76° 15.139'
Found in the park by Lewis St. in Perth

Leeds and Grenville County

Jones Falls Waste Weir, Eastern Region, Leeds and Grenville County,
Jones Falls
Water control, Rideau River, Rating: 1/4, Access: Easy
GPS Location: N 44° 32.856' W 76° 14.298'
A control which has obliterated Jones Falls

Lennox and Addington County

Babcock Mill Cascade, Eastern Region, Lennox County, Odessa
Cascade Type, Not known, Rating: 2/4, Access: Easy
GPS Location: N 44° 16.362' W 76° 43.141'
100 Bridge Street in Odessa by Babcock Mill

Buttermilk Falls (Forest Mills), Eastern Region, Lennox and
Addington County, Forest Mills
Cascade Type, Salmon River, Rating: 2/4, Access: Easy
GPS Location: N 44° 20.064' W 77° 02.832'
Found about 0.5 km west of Forest Mills on ON-12

Crooked Slide, Eastern Region, Lennox County, Combermere

Cascade Type, Rockingham Creek, Rating: 1/4, Access: Easy
GPS Location: N 45° 22.25' W 77° 36.876'
Off Old Barry's Bay Road just north of Combermere

Flinton Falls, Eastern Region, Lennox and Addington County,
Flinton
Cascade Type, Skootamatta River, Rating: 2/4, Access: Easy
GPS Location: N 44° 41.449' W 77° 12.742'
Near the north end of Flinton Rd in Flinton

Forest Mills Falls, Eastern Region, Lennox and Addington County,
Forest Mills
Cascade Type, Salmon River, Rating: 2/4, Access: Easy
GPS Location: N 44° 20.064' W 77° 02.832'
Off Buttermilk Falls Rd. west of Forest Mills

Millhaven Falls, Eastern Region, Lennox and Addington County, Millhaven
Plunge Type, Millhaven Creek, Rating: 2/4, Access: Easy
GPS Location: N 44° 11.777' W 76° 44.499'
Near Bath Rd and ON-4 in Millhaven

Napanee Falls, Eastern Region, Lennox and Addington County, Greater Napanee

Step Type, Napanee River, Rating: 2/4, Access: Easy
GPS Location: N 44° 15.041 W 76° 56.730
Off Dundas St E south of Napanee River

Newburgh Falls, Eastern Region, Lennox and Addington County, Newburgh
Cascade Type, Napanee River, Rating: 1/4, Access: Easy
GPS Location: N 44° 19.476' W 76° 52.440'
In Newburgh NE of Earl St.

Yarker Falls, Eastern Region, Lennox and Addington County, Yarker
Cascade Type, Napanee River, Rating: 2/4, Access: Easy
GPS Location: N 44° 22.281' W 76° 46.223'
In the middle of Yarker off County Rd 6

Northumberland County

Canpbellford Rapids (Crowe Bay Rapids), Eastern Region,
Northumberland County, Canpbellford
Rapids Type, Trent-Severn Canal, Rating: 1/4, Access: Easy
GPS Location: N 44° 20.0939' W 77° 46.355'
North on County Rd 38/Front St. from Canpbellford for 3.8 km

Crowe Bridge Rapids, Eastern Region, Northumberland County,
Campbellford
Rapids Type, Crowe River, Rating: 2/4, Access: Easy
GPS Location: N 44° 22.848' W 77° 45.318'
On Crowe River Rd 12 km north of Campbellford

Healey Falls , Eastern Region

Type: Step Type
River and County: Trent River, Healey Falls, Northumberland County
GPS Location: N 44° 22.55' W 77° 46.867'
Rating: 3/4
Access: Easy, 2 Minutes

Description: A very pleasant place to visit, and apparently good for fishing as well. Fine spot for a family outing.

Getting There: From County Rd 50 near the village of Healey Falls, take a small access road just north of the bridge going over the Trent. Don't take Coles Point Rd. which is nearby but look for an unmarked road closer to the bridge. There is parking just above the falls.

Photography Tips: There is a path that will bring you to river level which offers some great wide views.

Nearby Attractions: The Crowe Bridge and Campbellford Rapids are nearby although both are mediocre.

Ranney Falls, Eastern Region, Northumberland County, Canpbellford
Cascade Type, Trent River, Rating: 2/4, Access: Easy
GPS Location: N 44° 17.694' W 77° 48.108'
Found at the west side of Ferris Provincial Park

Ottawa-Carleton County

Cardinal Creek Falls, Eastern Region, Ottawa-Carleton County, Orleans
Cascade Type, Cardinal Creek, Rating: 1/4, Access: Easy
GPS Location: N 45° 29.132' W 75° 28.081'
Off Walter's Rd in Orleans

Chat Falls, Eastern Region, Ottawa-Carleton County, Fitzroy Harbour
Dam, Ottawa River, Rating: 1/4, Access: None
GPS Location: N 45° 28.970' W 76° 12.537'
Obliterated by dam in 1931

Chaudiere Falls, Eastern Region, Ottawa-Carleton County, Ottawa
Plunge Type, Ottawa River, Rating: 2/4, Access: Easy
GPS Location: N 45° 25.229' W 75° 43.070'
Can be viewed from the Chaudieres Bridge/Booth Street

Fitzroy Cascade, Eastern Reg, Ottawa-Carleton Cty, Fitzroy Harbour
Cascade Type, Carp River, Rating: 1/4, Access: Easy
GPS Location: N 45° 28.970' W 76° 12.537'
Found in the Fitzroy Provincial Park

Fitzroy Falls, Eastern Region, Ottawa-Carleton County, Fitzroy Harbour
Cascade Type, Carp River, Rating: 2/4, Access: Easy
GPS Location: N 45° 28.970' W 76° 12.537'
Found in the Fitzroy Provincial Park

Galetta Falls, Eastern Region, Ottawa-Carleton County, Galetta
Cascade Type, Mississippi River, Rating: 1/4, Access: Obstructed
GPS Location: N 45° 25.665' W 76° 15.149'
In Galetta at Galetta Side Road where it crosses the Trent River

Orleans Falls, Eastern Region, Ottawa-Carleton County, Orleans
Plunge Type, Taylor Creek, Rating: 2/4, Access: Moderate
GPS Location: N 45° 29.250' W 75° 29.338'
In Orleans off St. Joseph Blvd west of Trim Rd.

Rideau Falls, Eastern Ontario Region

Type: Curtain Type
River and County: Rideau River, Ottawa, Ottawa-Carleton County
GPS Location: N 45°26.4' W 75° 41.8'

Rating: 3/4
Access: Easy, 2 Minutes

Description:
Usually a falls looks better in a natural setting but I think in this instance the background of the Ottawa River and the capital city enhance the view.

Getting There:
Get onto Sussex Drive heading east, as it parallels the Ottawa River. When you cross over a bridge spanning the Rideau River, look for a parking lot on your left. A short trail brings you to the falls.

Photography Tips: Images across the top which include the Ottawa River can be interesting.

Nearby Attractions: The City of Ottawa is a great place to visit. The area near this falls is not far from the Prime Minister's official Residence as well as the Governor-General's at Rideau Hall.

The Hog's Back (Prince of Wales Falls), Eastern Region

Type: Cascade and Plunge type
River and County: Rideau River, Ottawa, Ottawa-Carleton County
GPS Location: N 45° 22.321' W 75° 41.749'

Rating: 3/4
Access: Moderate, 10 Minute

Description: This area was part of the Trent Canal System and has
been extensively changed from its original state. The central channel
was dug to accommodate large spring flows but it has a natural look.
The dam's upstream was a very challenging construction and it
collapsed three times before successfully being completed.

Getting There: From Regional Rd 69 going north into Ottawa, take
Meadowlands Dr. East to the east, for about 1.5 km. After you cross
the Rideau Canal, look for an immediate left bringing you into a
parking area.

Photography Tips: Leave yourself some time to explore the area. The
rock slabs across the river from where you park allow multiple
interesting views.

Nearby Attractions: The Rideau Falls is only about a half hour drive.

Peterborough County

Burleigh Falls, Eastern Region, Peterborough County, Burleigh Falls
Plunge Type, River, Rating: 2/4, Access: Easy
GPS Location: N 44° 33.372' W 78° 12.144'
Just south of Burleigh Falls off ON-28

Haultain Cascade, Eastern Region, Peterborough County, Apsley
Cascade Type, Eels Creek, Rating: 1/4, Access: Easy
GPS Location: N 44° 38.580' W 78° 08.135'
11.7 kmm south of Apsley on ON-28

High Falls (Apsley), Eastern Region, Peterborough County, Apsley
Cascade Type, River, Rating: 1/4, Access: Moderate
GPS Location: N 44° 48.216' W 78° 05.814'
North of Apsley 1 km se of Everett Rd

High Falls (Eels), Eastern Region, Peterborough County, Burleigh Falls
Cascade Type, Eels Creek, Rating: 2/4, Access: Difficult
GPS Location: N 44° 35.850' W 78° 05.305'
Canoe or extended hike

Marble Rapids, Eastern Region, Peterborough County, Cloyne
Rapids Type, Marble lake, Rating: 1/4, Access: Easy
GPS Location: N 44° 50.118' W 77° 08.225'
Marble Lake Rd and Highway 506 NE of Cloyne

Mississauga Cascade, Eastern Region, Peterborough County, Bobcaygeon
Cascade Type, Mississauga River, Rating: 1/4, Access: Easy
GPS Location: N 44° 40.470' W 78° 20.928'
Off Mississauga Dam Rd west of REG-507

North River Cascade, Eastern Region, Peterborough County, Havelock
Cascade Type, North River, Rating: 2/4, Access: Easy
GPS Location: N 44° 30.328' W 77° 50.342'
Off Preston Rd NE of Havelock

Perry's Creek Cascade, Eastern Region, Peterborough County, Burleigh Falls
Cascade Type, Perry's Creek, Rating: 1/4, Access: Easy
GPS Location: N 44° 33.679' W 78° 12.622'
In Burleigh Falls off Hwy-28 south of Hwy 36

South Eels Cascade, Eastern Region, Peterborough County, Burleigh Falls
Cascade Type, Eels Creek, Rating: 2/4, Access: Easy
GPS Location: N 44° 35.215' W 78° 04.224'
Off Northey's Bay Rd west of County Rd 6

Three Bears Rapids, Eastern Region, Peterborough County, Burleigh Falls
Rapids Type, Eels Creek, Rating: 1/4, Access: Difficult
GPS Location: N 44° 36.437' W 78° 05.944'
Canoe or extended hike

Warsaw Caves Falls, Eastern Region, Peterborough County, Warsaw
Irregular Cascade Type, Indian River, Rating: 1/4, Access: Easy
GPS Location: N 44° 27.715' W 78° 07.488'
In Warsaw Caves Conservation Area

Prescott and Russell County

High Falls (Casselman), Eastern Region, Prescott and Russell
County, Cassellman
Plunge Type, South Nation River, Rating: 1/4, Access: Easy
GPS Location: N 45° 19.065' W 75° 05.593'
Off Principale St at north of Cassellman

Jessups Falls, Eastern Region, Prescott and Russell County, Jessups
Falls
Dam, South Nation River, Rating: 1/4, Access: Easy
GPS Location: N 45° 33.630' W 75° 03.570'
Obliterated by dam

Renfrew County

Aumonds Rapids, Eastern Region, Renfrew County, Palmer Rapids
Rapids Type, Madawaska River, Rating: 1/4, Access: Easy
GPS Location: N 45° 16.854' W 77° 25.289'
Off Homestead Rd 6 km from Palmer Rd.

Barron Canyon Rd Falls, Eastern Region, Renfrew County,
Algonquin Park
Plunge Type, Not known, Rating: 2/4, Access: Moderate
GPS Location: N 45° 53.686' W 77° 39.588'
Off Barron Canyon Road 40 km from Trans Canada

Bonnechere Falls (First Chute), Eastern Region

Type: Cascade Type
River and County: Bonnechere River, Renfrew, Renfrew County
GPS Location: N 45° 29.933' W 76° 33.65'

Rating: 3/4
Access: Moderate, 10 Minutes

Description:
There was a series of five waterfalls along the Bonnechere River that
loggers bypassed with wooden chutes. Thus the original name for
Bonnechere Falls was First Chute. There are no traces of this now and
it is a very natural setting which you will likely have all to yourself.

Getting There:
From the Town of Refrew, take Hwy 60 East and turn right on Trans-
Canada Hwy/ON-17 E. After 2.5 km. turn left at County Road 6 (signs
for Lochwinnoch Road), and after another 2.1 km., make a left at
Thompson Rd. After about 3.9 km, you will see a parking area on the
left. Follow a trail near the back which makes its way down to the river
and the falls.
Photography Tips: Their are excellent spots to set up along the length
of this long cascade. Views looking downstream may offer the most
and panoramic images are interesting.
Nearby Attractions:
Third Chute is about 45 minutes by car.

Exam Time Rapids, Eastern Region, Renfrew County, Bruceton
Rapids Type, River, Rating: 1/4, Access: Moderate
GPS Location: N 45° 14.118' W 77° 20.838'
Canoe

Fifth Chute, Eastern Region, Renfrew County, Eganville
Dam Type, Bonnechere River, Rating: 1/4, Access: Easy
GPS Location: N 45° 32.374' W 77° 05.887'
Obliterated by dam

Fourth Chute Lower, Eastern Ontario Region

Type: Cascade Type
River and County: Bonnechere River, Fourth Chute, Renfrew County
GPS Location: N 45° 30.2' W 77°00.42'
Rating: 3/4
Access: Easy, 1 Minute

Description:
This is a great destination, especially for photographers. There is a layer
of rock at river level which allows you to walk about and find
wonderful images.

Getting There:
From Highway 60 at Eganville, go south on Fourth Chute Rd. for about 9 km. After you cross the bridge over the Bonnechere River, you will find parking on the right side.

Photography Tips:
If you make your way with care onto the layer of rock at river level, you will find many interesting elements to use in the foreground and background against the water. Look for grasses and colorful rock layers. Panoramas are available.

Nearby Attractions:
The upper Fourth Chute is on the other side of the road, and a commercial attraction for Scenic Caves is on the other side of the bridge.

Fourth Chute Upper, Eastern Ontario Region

Type: Cascade Type
River and County: Bonnechere River, Fourth Chute, Renfrew County
GPS Location: N 45° 30.2' W 77°00.42'

Rating: 3/4
Access: Easy, 1 Minute

Description: This is a great destination, especially for photographers. There is a layer of rock at river level which allows you to walk about and find wonderful images.

Getting There: From Highway 60 at Eganville, go south on Fourth Chute Rd. for about 9 km. After you cross the bridge over the Bonnechere River, you will find parking on the right side.

Photography Tips: You can get in tight to the edge of the water for some interesting views. Use a wide lens.

Nearby Attractions: The Lower Fourth Chute is on the other side of the road, and a commercial attraction for Scenic Caves is on the other side of the bridge.

Grants Creek Falls, Eastern Region, Renfrew County, Mattawa
Cascade Type, Grants Creek, Rating: 2/4, Access: Difficult
GPS Location: N 46° 11.751' W 77° 56.511'
South of Hwy-17 east of Mattawa. Extended hike

Hyland Falls, Eastern Region, Renfrew County, Griffith
Cascade Type, Madawaska River, Rating: 2/4, Access: Easy
GPS Location: N 45° 15.174' W 77° 11.607'
By Hyland Creek Rd off ON-41 near Griffith

Jacks Chute Rapids, Eastern Region, Renfrew County, Bonnechere
Rapids Type, Bonnechere River, Rating: 1/4, Access: Easy
GPS Location: N 45° 40.488' W 77° 35.418'
End of Jack Chute Rd off Hwy-58

Old Killahoe Cascade, Eastern Region, Renfrew County, Old Killahoe
Cascade Type, Brennans Creek, Rating: 1/4, Access: Easy
GPS Location: N 45° 32.112' W 77° 24.898'
Found beside the old mill in Old Killahoe

Pakenham Falls, Eastern Region, Renfrew County, Pakenham
Cascade Type, Mississippi River, Rating: 2/4, Access: Easy
GPS Location: N 45° 20.139' W 76° 17.163'
By the 5 Arch stone bridge, Kinburn Side Rd, Pakenham

Rifle Chute, Eastern Region, Renfrew County, Bruceton
Chute Type, Madawaska River, Rating: 1/4, Access: Moderate
GPS Location: N 45° 14.024' W 77° 20.598'
1 Km off Hyland Creek Rd in Lower Madawaska River P.P.

Second Chute, Eastern Region, Renfrew County, Renfrew
Cascade Type, Bonnechere River, Rating: 2/4, Access: Easy
GPS Location: N 45° 28.637' W 76° 41.445'
Off ON-60 in Renfrew

Slate Falls, Eastern Region, Renfrew County, Palmer Rapids
Cascade Type, Madawaska River, Rating: 2/4, Access: Moderate
GPS Location: N 45° 14.159' W 77° 16.422'
1 Km off Hyland Creek Rd in Lower Madawaska River P.P.

Split Rock Rapids, Eastern Region, Renfrew County, Palmer Rapids
Rapids Type, Madawaska River, Rating: 1/4, Access: Easy
GPS Location: N 45° 13.766' W 77° 20.186'
1 Km off Hyland Creek Rd in Lower Madawaska River P.P.

Third Chute, Eastern Region, Renfrew County, Douglas
Cascade Type, Bonnechere River, Rating: 1/4, Access: Easy
GPS Location: N 45°30.466' W 76° 56.15'
Off Emelin St in Douglas

Mystery Falls, Eastern Region, Renfrew County, Bancroft
Cascade Type, Unknown River, Rating: 2/4, Access: Moderate
GPS Location: N 45° 12.363' W 77° 13.585'
An unnamed falls along Hwy-41

Conroy Rapids, Eastern Region, Renfrew County, Palmer Rapids
Rapids Type, York River, Rating: 1/4, Access: Easy
GPS Location: N 45° 15.007' W 77° 37.968'
Near Pinecrest and Spence Rds SW of Palmer Rapids

Northeast Region

Cochrane County

Kapkigiwan Falls, Northeast Region, Cochrane County, Kap-Kig-Iwan P.P.
Cascade Type, Kapkigiwan River , Rating: 3/4, Access: Difficult
GPS Location: N 47° 47.779' W 79° 53.180'
Found in Kap-Kig-Iwan P.P. (Closed)

Keneki Lake Falls, Northeast Region, Cochrane County
Cascade Type, Keneki Lake, Rating: 1/4, Access: Difficult
GPS Location: N 48° 06.033' W 81° 55.982'
Canoe

New Post Falls, Northeast Region, Cochrane County, Lake Abitibi P.P.
Cascade Type, River, Rating: 4/4, Access: Easy
GPS Location: N 49° 59.437' W 81° 31.855'
Canoe

Sandy Falls, Northeast Region, Cochrane County, Timmins
Cascade Type, Mattagami River, Rating: 2/4, Access: Easy
GPS Location: N 48° 30.711' W 81° 26.584'
Off north end Maloney Rd, Timmins

Thunder House Falls, Northeast Region, Cochrane County, Hearst
Cascade Type, Missinaibi River, Rating: 3/4, Access: Difficult
GPS Location: N 50° 03.126' W 83° 11.028'
Canoe

Wawaitan Falls, Northeast Region, Cochrane County
Cascade Type, Mattagami River, Rating: 2/4, Access: Difficult
GPS Location: N 48° 20.678' W 81° 29.611'
Off Wawaitan Rd N from outlet to Kenogamissi Lake

Manitoulin County

Bridal Veil Falls (Kagawong)
Cottage Country Region
Type: Plunge Type
River and County: Kagawong River, Kagawong, Manitoulin County
GPS Location: N 45° 54.028' W 82° 15.391'

Rating: 3/4
Access: Easy trail difficulty, 2 Minutes

Description: This is a great looking falls, a large plunge type. It looks great in winter as well with a large ice cone forming below.
Getting There: The Main Street (ON-540) of Kagawong passes by the signed entrance of Bridal Veil Falls
Photography Tips: You need to pick well to find an unobstructed view, there is a nice wide view near the top as you leave the parking lot.

High Falls (Manitoulin), Northeast Region, Manitoulin County, Manitowaning

Plunge Type, Francis Brook, Rating: 2/4, Access: Easy
GPS Location: N 45° 47.996' W 81° 51.197'
Off On-6 7.6 km north of Manitowaning

Nipissing County

Allen Rapids, Northeast Region, Nipissing County, Algonquin Park
P.P.
Rapids Type, Nipissing River, Rating: 1/4, Access: Difficult
GPS Location: N 45° 53.004' W 78° 48.977'
Canoe or extended hike

Battery Rapids, Northeast Region, Nipissing County, Algonquin P.P.
Rapids Type, Barron River, Rating: 1/4, Access: Difficult
GPS Location: N 45° 59.052' W 78° 15.090'
Canoe

Bingham Chute, Northeast Region, Parry Sound County, Powassan
Cascade Type, French River, Rating: 2/4, Access: Easy
GPS Location: N 46° 04.508' W 79° 23.872'
Dam, Off ON-534 in Powassan

Carcajou Falls, Northeast Region, Nipissing County, Algonquin P.P.
Cascade Type, Carcajou Creek, Rating: 2/4, Access: Difficult
GPS Location: N 45° 50.010' W 77° 46.608'
Canoe

Cascade Rapids, Northeast Region, Nipissing County, Algonquin
P.P.
Rapids Type, Barron River, Rating: 1/4, Access: Difficult
GPS Location: N 45° 58.770' W 78° 13.692'
Canoe

Cedar Lake Falls, Northeast Region, Nipissing County, Algonquin
Park P.P.
Cascade Type, Cedar Lake, Rating: 3/4, Access: Difficult
GPS Location: N 46° 00.309' W 78° 29.066'
Canoe

Crooked Chute, Northeast Region, Nipissing County, Eau Claire
Cascade Type, Amable du Fond River, Rating: 2/4, Access: Easy
GPS Location: N 46° 16.648' W 78° 55.013'
From Transcanada Highway/ Ontario-17 go south on On-630 for 1
km.

Crow River Falls, Northeast Region, Nipissing County, Algonquin Park P.P.
Cascade Type, Crow River, Rating: 2/4, Access: Difficult
GPS Location: N 45° 57.347' W 78° 11.142'
Canoe

Crystal Falls, Northeast Region, Nipissing County, Sturgeon Falls Dam, Sturgeon River, Rating: 1/4, Access: Easy
GPS Location: N 46° 19.233' W 79° 58.266'
Obliterated by dam

Devils Cellar Rapids, Northeast Region, Nipissing County, Algonquin P.P.
Rapids Type, Petawawa River, Rating: 2/4, Access: Difficult
GPS Location: N 45° 57.019' W 78° 05.532'
Canoe

Devils Chute, Northeast Region, Nipissing County, Algonquin P.P.
Rapids Type, Petawawa River, Rating: 2/4, Access: Difficult
GPS Location: N 46° 01.001' W 78° 21.977'
Canoe

Duchesnay Falls (East and West)

Northeast Region
Type: Cascade Type
River and County: Duchesnay River, North Bay, Nipissing County
GPS Location: N 46° 20.053' W 79° 30.561'

Rating: 4/4
Access: Moderate trail difficulty, 10 Minutes

Description: A magnificent set of falls which are easy to visit and offer a wide variety of vistas to explore. Plan to have at least a few hours here.
Getting There: Found by the Transcanada Hwy/ON-17 at the west end of North Bay. Look for signs and parking lot.
Photography Tips: There are trails which parallel the course of both falls which will bring you to a great many good spots to set up. Look also for fine images at the base.

Eau Claire Gorge Falls

Northeast Region
Type: Cascade Type

River and County: Amable du Fond River, Eau Claire Gorge
Conservation Area, Nipissing County
GPS Location: N 46° 15.359' W 78° 55.029'
Rating: 4/4
Access: Moderate trail difficulty, 10 Minutes

Description: One of Ontario's finest waterfalls. The river travels
through a steep gorge in this section and the result is a wild piece of
water in a natural setting.
Getting There: Go south on ON-630 off ON-17 east of North Bay
and after 5 km turn right on Peddler's Drive. The entrance to the Eau
Claire Gorge Conservation Area is a short distance. There is a trail map
in the parking lot.
Photography Tips: With care you can find open vantage points on the
sides of the gorge but you need to be very cautious.

Galipo River Falls, Northeast Region, Nipissing County, Town
Cascade Type, Galipo River, Rating: 2/4, Access: Difficult
GPS Location: N 45° 25.982' W 78° 22.897'
Canoe only

Gravelle Chute, Northeast Region, Nipissing County
Overfalls Type, Amable du Fond River, Rating: 1/4, Access: Moderate
GPS Location: N 46° 08.778' W 78° 56.048'
Off ON-630, Canoe or hike

Grillade Rapids, Northeast Region, Nipissing County, Algonquin P.P.
Rapids Type, Lake Travers, Rating: 1/4, Access: Moderate
GPS Location: N 45° 57.906' W 78° 02.160'
East side of Lake Travers, Canoe

Gut Rapids, Northeast Region, Nipissing County, Algonquin P.P.
Rapids Type, York River, Rating: 1/4, Access: Difficult
GPS Location: N 45° 13.013' W 78° 09.972'
South end of Algonquin P.P., Canoe

High Chute, Northeast Region, Nipissing County, L'Amable
Chute Type, Madawaska River, Rating: 1/4, Access: Difficult
GPS Location: N 45° 30.540' W 78° 07.685'
Canoe

High Falls (Barron), Northeast Region, Nipissing County, Algonquin P.P.
Cascade Type, Barron River, Rating: 4/4, Access: Difficult
GPS Location: N 45° 51.529' W 77° 41.531'
Canoe or extended hike

High Falls (Little Bonnechere River), Northeast Region, Nipissing County, Algonquin P.P.
Cascade Type, Little Bonnechere River, Rating: 3/4, Access: Difficult
GPS Location: N 45° 43.188' W 77° 53.088'
Canoe or extended hike

High Falls (Nipissing River), Northeast Region, Nipissing County, Algonquin P.P.
Cascade Type, Nipissing River, Rating: 2/4, Access: Difficult
GPS Location: N 45° 54.375' W 78° 44.670'
Canoe

Laurel Lake Falls, Northeast Region, Nipissing County, Algonquin P.P.
Cascade Type, Cauchon Creek, Rating: 2/4, Access: Difficult
GPS Location: N 46° 03.419' W 78° 37.220'
Canoe or extended hike

Lion Chute, Northeast Region, Nipissing County, Mattawa
Overfalls Type, Antoine Creek, Rating: 1/4, Access: Moderate
GPS Location: N 46° 21.007' W 78° 51.977'
Canoe

Long Rapids, Northeast Region, Nipissing County, Madawaska
Rapids Type, Madawaska River, Rating: 1/4, Access: Difficult
GPS Location: N 45° 30.528' W 78° 07.772'
Canoe

Mew Lake Cascade, Northeast Region, Nipissing County, Algonquin P.P.
Cascade Type, Madawaska River, Rating: 1/4, Access: Moderate
GPS Location: N 45° 34.048' W 78° 30.766'
Canoe or hike

North Tea Falls, Northeast Region, Nipissing County, Algonquin P.P.
Cascade Type, Tea Lake, Rating: 2/4, Access: Difficult
GPS Location: N 45° 58.315' W 78° 59.466'
Canoe

Observatory Falls, Northeast Region, Nipissing County, Algonquin P.P.
Rapids Type, Petawawa River, Rating: 1/4, Access: Moderate
GPS Location: N 45° 57.594' W 78° 03.996'
Off Achray Rd in Algonquin P.P.

Palmer Rapids, Northeast Region, Nipissing County, Jewelville
Rapids Type, Madawaska River, Rating: 2/4, Access: Moderate
GPS Location: N 45° 19.763' W 77° 32.453'
Off Dam Road west of Jewelville

Paresseaux Falls, Northeast Region, Nipissing County, Mattawa
Cascade Type, Mattawa River, Rating: 3/4, Access: Difficult
GPS Location: N 46° 18.124' W 78° 58.339'
Canoe

Peddler's Falls, Northeast Region, Nipissing County

Cascade Type, Trib Amable du Fond River, Rating: 2/4, Access: Moderate
GPS Location: N 46° 15.619' W 78° 50.875'
Just east of the Eau Claire Gorge Falls entrance

Pen-to-Rock Falls, Northeast Region, Nipissing County, Algonquin P.P.
Cascade Type, Pen Lake, Rating: 2/4, Access: Difficult
GPS Location: N 45° 28.718' W 78° 23.771'
Canoe

Petit Paresseaux Falls, Northeast Region, Nipissing County, Mattawa
Overfalls Type, Mattawa River, Rating: 2/4, Access: Difficult
GPS Location: N 46° 18.006' W 78° 57.977'
Canoe, south of Paresseaux Falls

Red Pine Chute, Northeast Region, Nipissing County, Mattawa P.P.
Overfalls Type, Kaibuskong River, Rating: 2/4, Access: Moderate
GPS Location: N 46° 17.004' W 79° 04.973'
Canoe

Sandy Falls (Sturgeon River), Northeast Region, Nipissing County, Evansville
Cascade Type, Sturgeon River, Rating: 2/4, Access: Moderate
GPS Location: N 46° 23.788' W 79° 51.783'
Canoe

Shirley Lake Falls, Northeast Region, Nipissing County, Algonquin P.P.
Cascade Type, Shirley Lake, Rating: 2/4, Access: Moderate
GPS Location: N 45° 40.154' W 78° 06.155'
Canoe

Squirrel Rapids, Northeast Region, Nipissing County, Algonquin P.P.
Rapids Type, Barron River, Rating: 1/4, Access: Difficult
GPS Location: N 45° 59.005' W 78° 15.974'
Canoe

Sturgeon Falls, Northeast Region, Nipissing County, Sturgeon Falls Dam, Sturgeon River, Rating: 1/4, Access: Easy
GPS Location: N 46° 22.089' W 79° 55.963'
Obliterated by dam.

Talon Chute, Northeast Region, Nipissing Cty, Blanchard's Landing Chute Type, Mattawa River, Rating: 2/4, Access: Difficult
GPS Location: N 46° 16.952' W 79° 00.204'
Canoe

White Horse Rapids, Northeast Region, Nipissing County, Algonquin P.P.
Rapids Type, Barron River, Rating: 1/4, Access: Difficult
GPS Location: N 45° 58.770' W 78° 13.692'
Canoe

Parry Sound County

Big Jameson Rapids, Northeast Region, Parry Sound County, French River P.P.
Rapids Type, French River, Rating: 1/4, Access: Moderate
GPS Location: N 45° 55.986' W 80° 58.788'
Canoe

Big Parisien Rapids, Northeast Region, Parry Sound County, French River P.P.
Rapids Type, French River, Rating: 1/4, Access: Moderate
GPS Location: N 46° 03.012' W 80° 14.604'
Canoe

Big Pine Rapids, Northeast Region, Parry Sound County, French River P.P.
Rapids Type, French River, Rating: 1/4, Access: Moderate
GPS Location: N 46° 04.068' W 80° 12.328'
Canoe

Bingham Chute, Northeast Region, Parry Sound County, Powassan Cascade Type, French River, Rating: 2/4, Access: Easy
GPS Location: N 46° 04.508' W 79° 23.872'
Dam, Off ON-534 in Powassan

Blue Chute, Northeast Region, Parry Sound County, French River P.P.
Rapids Type, French River, Rating: 1/4, Access: Moderate
GPS Location: N 46° 03.223' W 80° 12.576'
Canoe

Broadbent Falls, Northeast Region, Parry Sound County, McKellar
Cascade Type, Little Seguin River, Rating: 2/4, Access: Moderate
GPS Location: N 45° 28.148' W 79° 49.622'
Off Broadbent Road south east of McKellar

Brooks Falls

Northeast Region
Type: Cascade Type
River and County: Magnetawan River, Emsdale, Parry Sound
GPS Location: N 45° 33.352' W 79° 17.734'
Rating: 3/4
Access: Moderate difficulty, 2 Minute
Description: Located in Brooks Falls Park near Emsdale, this is an excellent falls found in a natural setting. When I visited in April during the spring melt, it was looking very powerful. At dryer times of the year, it may be more subdued.

Getting There: From Highway 11, north of Emsdale, take Deer Lake Rd. Exit and go east for about 3.5 km. You will see signs for Brook Falls Park. There is parking by the river and the trail to the falls is from this lot. It is short but moderately steep in spots.
Photography Tips:
You can find good setup spots from the base to the crest with excellent foreground elements available.
Nearby Attractions: Stubbs Falls in Arrowhead Provincial Park is less than a half an hour drive to the south on Highway 11.

Bunny Trail Falls, Northeast Region, Parry Sound Cty, Waubamik
Cascade Type, Unknown River, Rating: 2/4, Access: Easy
GPS Location: N 45° 33.756' W 80° 02.265'
Off Bunny Trail Rd 12.6 km north of ON-24

Burks Falls, Northeast Region, Parry Sound County, Burks Falls
Dam, Magnetawan River, Rating: 2/4, Access: Easy
GPS Location: N 45° 37.186' W 79° 24.735'
Obliterated by dam

Chapmans Chute, Northeast Region, Parry Sound County, Chapman's Landing
Chute Type, South River, Rating: 1/4, Access: Moderate
GPS Location: N 46° 06.182' W 79° 31.116'
Off Chapman's Landing Rd.

Cody Rapids, Northeast Region, Parry Sound County, Maple Island
Rapids Type, Magnetawan River, Rating: 2/4, Access: Easy
GPS Location: N 45° 33.756' W 80° 02.265'
Off Nelson Clelland Rd 2 km. east of ON-520

Corkery Falls, Northeast Region, Parry Sound County, Powassan
Dam, South River, Rating: 1/4, Access: Moderate
GPS Location: N 46° 00.087' W 79° 25.512'
Obliterated by dam

Cox Chute, Northeast Region, Parry Sound County, South River
Chute Type, South River, Rating: 1/4, Access: Moderate
GPS Location: N 45° 54.744' W 79° 25.092'
Canoe

Crooked Rapids (French River), Northeast Region, Parry Sound
County, French River P.P.
Rapids Type, French River, Rating: 1/4, Access: Moderate
GPS Location: N 46° 02.544' W 80° 16.074'
Canoe

Davidson Chute, Northeast Region, Parry Sound County, South River
Chute Type, South River, Rating: 1/4, Access: Moderate
GPS Location: N 45° 55.266' W 79° 25.158'
Canoe

Devils Chute (French River), Northeast Region, Parry Sound
County, French River P.P.
Rapids Type, French River, Rating: 1/4, Access: Moderate
GPS Location: N 46° 03.012' W 80° 14.604'
Canoe

Devils Door Rapids, Northeast Region, Parry Sound County, French
River P.P.
Rapids Type, French River, Rating: 1/4, Access: Moderate
GPS Location: N 45° 56.226' W 80° 58.464'
Canoe

Double Rapids, Northeast Region, Parry Sound County, French River
P.P.
Rapids Type, French River, Rating: 1/4, Access: Moderate
GPS Location: N 46° 03.606' W 80° 12.954'
Canoe

Dutchman Chutes, Northeast Region, Parry Sound County, Arnstein
Chute Type, Pickerel River, Rating: 1/4, Access: Moderate
GPS Location: N 45° 52.002' W 79° 55.977'
Canoe

Elliott Chute, Northeast Region, Parry Sound County, South River
Dam, South River, Rating: 1/4, Access: Moderate
GPS Location: N 46° 03.624' W 79° 23.364'
Obliterated by dam

Fagan Falls, Northeast Region, Parry Sound County, Ahmic Harbour

Waterfall Type, Magnetawan River, Rating: 2/4, Access: Easy
GPS Location: N 45° 40.079' W 79° 44.466'
Dam at top, off Robinson Rd.

Five Mile Rapids, Northeast Region, Parry Sound County, French
River P.P.
Rapids Type, French River, Rating: 1/4, Access: Moderate
GPS Location: N 46° 02.460' W 80° 16.674'
Canoe

Freeman Chute, Northeast Region, Parry Sound County, South River
Chute Type, South River, Rating: 1/4, Access: Moderate
GPS Location: N 45° 57.714' W 79° 24.504'
Canoe

Geisler Chute, Northeast Region, Parry Sound County, South River
Chute Type, South River, Rating: 1/4, Access: Moderate
GPS Location: N 45° 58.782' W 79° 24.108'
Canoe

Gimball Chute, Northeast Region, Parry Sound County, South River
Chute Type, South River, Rating: 1/4, Access: Moderate
GPS Location: N 45° 53.454' W 79° 24.360'
Canoe

Hab Rapids, Northeast Region, Parry Sound County, McDougall
Rapids Type, Seguin River, Rating: 1/4, Access: Moderate
GPS Location: N 45° 24.050' W 79° 55.500'
Off Seguin Rd SE of McDougall

Herring Chutes, Northeast Region, Parry Sound County, French
River P.P.
Chute Type, French River, Rating: 1/4, Access: Moderate
GPS Location: N 45° 56.347' W 80° 58.626'
Canoe

Horseshoe Falls, Northeast Region, Parry Sound County, French
River P.P.
Cascade Type, French River, Rating: 2/4, Access: Moderate
GPS Location: N 45° 59.416' W 80° 28.777'
Canoe

Indian Rapids, Northeast Region, Parry Sound County, McDougall
Rapids Type, Seguin River, Rating: 1/4, Access: Moderate
GPS Location: N 45° 24.150' W 79° 54.360'
Canoe

Knoefli Falls, Northeast Region, Parry Sound County, Ahmic
Harbour
cascade Type, Magnetawan River, Rating: 2/4, Access: Easy
GPS Location: N 45° 39.966' W 79° 43.411'
Just south of ON-124 east of Ahmic Harbour

Liley Chute, Northeast Region, Parry Sound County, French River
P.P.
Chute Type, French River, Rating: 1/4, Access: Moderate
GPS Location: N 45° 56.347' W 80° 58.626'
Canoe

Little Jameson Rapids, Northeast Region, Parry Sound County,
French River P.P.
Rapids Type, French River, Rating: 1/4, Access: Moderate
GPS Location: N 45° 56.148' W 80° 58.584'
Canoe

Little Parisien Rapids, Northeast Region, Parry Sound County,
French River P.P.
Rapids Type, French River, Rating: 1/4, Access: Moderate
GPS Location: N 46° 03.096' W 80° 13.488'
Canoe

Little Pine Rapids, Northeast Region, Parry Sound County, French
River P.P.
Rapids Type, French River, Rating: 1/4, Access: Moderate
GPS Location: N 46° 04.410' W 80° 11.603'
Canoe

Lower Burnt Chute, Northeast Region, Parry Sound County,
Whitestone
Overfalls Type, Magnetawan River, Rating: 1/4, Access: Moderate
GPS Location: N 45° 43.457' W 79° 56.961'
Canoe

MacIndoo Falls, Northeast Region, Parry Sound County, Burk's Falls
Cascade Type, Magnetawan River, Rating: 2/4, Access: Moderate
GPS Location: N 45° 34.633' W 78° 28.919'
Canoe or extended hike

Magnetawan Lock, Northeast Region, Parry Sound County,
Magnetawan
Lock, Magnetawan River, Rating: 1/4, Access: Easy
GPS Location: N 45° 39.966' W 79° 43.411'
Obliterated by Lock

Mahzenazing Cascade, Northeast Region, Parry Sound County,
Collins Inlet
Rapids Type, Mahzenazing River, Rating: 1/4, Access: Easy
GPS Location: N 46° 00.276' W 81° 11.986'
Canoe

McNab Chute, Northeast Region, Parry Sound County, South River
Chute Type, South River, Rating: 1/4, Access: Moderate
GPS Location: N 46° 05.868' W 79° 28.626'
Canoe

Mountain Chute, Northeast Region, Parry Sound County, North
Magnetawan P.P.
Overfalls Type, Seguin River, Rating: 1/4, Access: Moderate
GPS Location: N 45° 45.456' W 80° 13.776'
Canoe

Needles Eye Rapids, Northeast Region, Nipissing County, Maple
Island
Rapids Type, Magnetawan River, Rating: 1/4, Access: Difficult
GPS Location: N 45° 43.404' W 79° 57.072'
Canoe

Old Man River Falls

Northeast Region
Type: cascade Type
River and County: Old Man River, Port Anson, Parry Sound
GPS Location: N 45° 36.982' W 79° 38.826'
Rating: 3/4

Access: Moderate trail difficulty, 5 Minutes

Description: A long cascade which meanders down a steep bank.
Getting There: From the town of Port Anson go west on Ahmic Lake
Road and the falls is to the south after 3.3 km
Photography Tips: It is difficult to find a view that is not obstructed by
brush but there are a couple of spots you need to search for.

Pickerel Lake Rd Cascade, Northeast Region, Parry Sound County,
Burks Falls
Curtain Type, Magnetawan River, Rating: 2/4, Access: Easy
GPS Location: N 45° 38.321' W 79° 24.381'
Off Pickerel Lake Rd. east of ON-11

Porter Rapids, Northeast Region, Parry Sound County, Dunchurch
Rapids Type, Magnetawan River, Rating: 1/4, Access: Moderate
GPS Location: N 45° 41.784' W 79° 51.054'
Canoe

Poverty Bay Chutes, Northeast Region, Parry Sound County, Ahmic
Harbour
Cascade Type, Magnetawan River, Rating: 2/4, Access: Easy
GPS Location: N 45° 41.132' W 79° 45.057'
Off Magnet Rd. north of Ahmic Harbour

Ragged Rapids (Manitouwabin), Northeast Region, Parry Sound
County, Hurdville
Rapids Type, Manitouwabin River, Rating: 1/4, Access: private
GPS Location: Private
Private

Recollet Falls
Northeast Region
Type: Irregular Step Type
River and County: French River, Alban, Parry Sound
GPS Location: N 46° 00.970' W 80° 35.101'
Rating: 3/4
Access: Moderate, 30 Minutes

Description: This is an interesting falls both in appearance and history. The falls were named after the Recollet Fathers who were the first white men to use the French River while they were engaged in missionary work in the early 1600's.

Getting There: On the Transcanada Highway/ HOn-69 about 45 minutes southeast of Sudbury French River provincial park is located along the river. Park in the lot there and look at the trails om the map. The trail to the falls is easy to find and takes about 30 minutes to reach the falls.

Photography Tips: There are excellent views across the face of the falls. In spring thaw look also for waterfalls coming off the cliffs.

Nearby Attractions: Meshaw Falls is about 15 minutes drive.

Restoule Falls, Northeast Region, Parry Sound County, Restoule
Cascade Type, Restoule River, Rating: 2/4, Access: Easy
GPS Location: N 46° 01.686' W 79° 43.181'
Off ON-534 just south of Olive St. in Restoule

Ross Rapids, Northeast Region, Parry Sound County, Dunchurch
Rapids Type, Magnetawan River, Rating: 1/4, Access: Moderate
GPS Location: N 45° 41.664' W 79° 47.826'
Canoe

Seller Rapids, Northeast Region, Parry Sound County, Dunchurch
Rapids Type, Magnetawan River, Rating: 1/4, Access: Moderate
GPS Location: N 45° 41.488' W 79° 46.652'
Canoe

Serpent Rapids, Northeast Region, Parry Sound County, McDougall
Rapids Type, Seguin River, Rating: 1/4, Access: Easy
GPS Location: N 45° 24.200' W 79° 54.067'
Canoe

South River Cascade, Northeast Region, Parry Sound County, South
River
Cascade Type, South River, Rating: 2/4, Access: Easy
GPS Location: N 45° 50.882' W 79° 22.515'
Off Mill Rd. in South River

Stirling Falls, Northeast Region, Parry Sound County, Stirling Falls
Cascade Type, Stirling Creek, Rating: 2/4, Access: Easy
GPS Location: N 45° 40.986' W 79° 25.902'
Off North Horn Lake Rd, in Stirling Falls

Stovepipe Rapids, Northeast Region, Parry Sound County, North
Magnetawan P.P.
Overfalls Type, Seguin River, Rating: 1/4, Access: Moderate
GPS Location: N 45° 45.696' W 80° 14.922'
Canoe

Thirty Dollar Rapids, Northeast Region, Parry Sound County,
Magnetawan River P.P.
Rapids Type, Magnetawan River, Rating: 1/4, Access: Moderate
GPS Location: N 45° 44.484' W 80° 20.910'
Canoe

Thompson Rapids, Northeast Region, Parry Sound County, Burk's
Falls
Rapids Type, Magnetawan River, Rating: 1/4, Access: Moderate
GPS Location: N 45° 38.290' W 79° 24.327'
Canoe

Truisler Chute, Northeast Region, Parry Sound County, South River
Chute Type, South River, Rating: 1/4, Access: Moderate
GPS Location: N 45° 57.924' W 79° 24.240'
Canoe

Upper Burnt Chute, Northeast Region, Parry Sound County, Whitestone
Chute Type, Magnetawan River, Rating: 1/4, Access: Moderate
GPS Location: N 45° 42.582' W 79° 54.900'
Canoe

Wasi Cascade, Northeast Region, Parry Sound County, Callander
Cascade Type, Wasi River, Rating: 1/4, Access: Easy
GPS Location: N 46° 11.859' W 79° 22.238'
Off Wasi Falls Rd. south of Callander

Wasi Falls, Northeast Region, Parry Sound County, Callander
Cascade Type, Wasi River, Rating: 3/4, Access: Easy
GPS Location: N 46° 11.957' W 79° 22.443'
Off Wasi Falls Rd. south of Callander

Sudbury County

Bear Chutes, Northeast Region, Sudbury County, Alban
Chute Type, Wanapitei River, Rating: 1/4, Access: Moderate
GPS Location: N 46° 05.742' W 80° 48.030'
Canoe

Cameron Falls, Northeast Region, Sudbury County, Massey
Dam, Aux Sables River, Rating: 1/4, Access: Moderate
GPS Location: N 46° 16.956' W 82° 09.006'
Obliterated by dam

Cascade Falls, Northeast Region, Sudbury County, Sudbury
Cascade Type, Vermillion River, Rating: 2/4, Access: Moderate
GPS Location: N 46° 26.099' W 81° 17.079'
Hike from the end of Inco Rd.

Centre Falls, Northeast Region, Sudbury County, Lady Evelyn
Smoothwater P.P.
Cascade Type, Lady Evelyn River, Rating: 3/4, Access: Moderate
GPS Location: N 47°17.672' W 80° 19.252'
Canoe

Chartrand Corners Falls, Northeast Region, Sudbury County,
Chartrand Corners
Cascade Type, Unknown River, Rating: 2/4, Access: Moderate
GPS Location: N 46° 08.074' W 80° 23.082'
From Chartrand Corners, west on Highway 64 for about 400 meters

Coniston Hydro Dam, Northeast Region, Sudbury County, Nickel
Centre

Cascade Type, Wanapitei River, Rating: 1/4, Access: Easy
GPS Location: N 46° 28.521' W 80° 49.244'
south on Coniston Hydro Rd, 800m from ON-17

Duncan Chute, Northeast Region, Sudbury County, Whitefish
Chute Type, Vermillion River, Rating: 1/4, Access: Moderate
GPS Location: N 46° 24.837' W 81° 18.639'
Canoe

Espanola Falls, Northeast Region, Sudbury County, Espanola
Dam, Spanish River, Rating: 1/4, Access: Easy
GPS Location: N 46° 16.198' W 81° 46.576'
Topped by a dam

Floodwood Chutes, Northeast Region, Sudbury County, Sturgeon
River P.P.
Cascade Type, Sturgeon River, Rating: 1/4, Access: Moderate
GPS Location: N 46° 41.538' W 80° 21.006'
Canoe

Frank Falls, Northeast Region, Sudbury County, Lady Evelyn
Smoothwater P.P.
Cascade Type, Lady Evelyn River, Rating: 3/4, Access: Moderate
GPS Location: N 47°18.360' W 80° 18.120'
Canoe

Gordon Chutes, Northeast Region, Sudbury County, Espanola
Rapids Type, Wakonassin River, Rating: 1/4, Access: Moderate
GPS Location: N 46° 29.932' W 81° 57.909'
Canoe

Helen Falls, Northeast Region, Sudbury County, Lady Evelyn
Smoothwater P.P.
Cascade Type, Lady Evelyn River, Rating: 3/4, Access: Moderate
GPS Location: N 47°13.170' W 80° 20.052'
Canoe

High Falls (Spanish River), Northeast Region, Sudbury County,
Whitefish
Dam, Spanish River, Rating: 1/4
GPS Location: N 46° 22.806' W 81° 33.946'
Obliterated by dam

Kenogamissi Falls, Northeast Region, Sudbury County, Timmins
Cascade Type, Mattagami River, Rating: 3/4, Access: Easy
GPS Location: N 48° 00.786' W 81° 33.462'
Off ON-144 south of Timmins

Kettle Falls, Northeast Region, Sudbury County, Sturgeon P.P.
Cascade Type, Sturgeon River, Rating: 3/4, Access: Moderate
GPS Location: N 47° 06.702' W 80° 41.688'
Canoe

Larchwood Cascade, Northeast Region, Sudbury County, Larchwood
Rapids Type, Vermillion River, Rating: 1/4, Access: Easy
GPS Location: N 46° 35.229' W 81° 18.375'
Off end of Morgan Rd. in Larchwood

Lorne Falls, Northeast Region, Sudbury County, Nairn

Cascade Type, Vermillion River, Rating: 2/4, Access: Easy
GPS Location: N 46° 19.024' W 81° 31.206'
Of end of Powerhouse Rd in Nairn

Lower Goose Falls, Northeast Region, Sudbury County, Sturgeon
River P.P.
Cascade Type, Sturgeon River, Rating: 1/4, Access: Moderate
GPS Location: N 46° 56.214' W 80° 25.884'
Canoe

Massey Chute, Northeast Region, Sudbury County, Massey
Rapids Type, Aux Sables River, Rating: 1/4, Access: Easy
GPS Location: N 46° 12.864' W 82° 04.272'
Off Sable St East

McCharles Lake Cascade, Northeast Region, Sudbury County, Whitefish
Rapids Type, Vermillion River, Rating: 1/4, Access: Moderate
GPS Location: N 46° 23.688' W 81° 16.854'
North of Graham Rd in Whitefish

McFadden Falls, Northeast Region, Sudbury County, Crean Hill
Cascade Type, Vermillion River, Rating: 2/4, Access: Moderate
GPS Location: N 46° 27.474' W 81° 17.052'
Canoe

McVittie Dam Falls, Northeast Region, Sudbury County, McVittie
Cascade Type, River, Rating: 1/4, Access: Easy
GPS Location: N 46° 17.163' W 80° 50.796'
Partially obliterated by hydro dam, McVittie Rd.

Meshaw Falls, Northeast Region, Sudbury County, Alban
Cascade Type, French River, Rating: 2/4, Access: Easy
GPS Location: N 46° 02.928' W 80° 34.167'
Off Dry Pine Bay Road, south of Alban

Nairn Falls, Northeast Region, Sudbury County, Nairn Centre
Dam Type, Spanish River, Rating: 2/4, Access: Easy
GPS Location: N 46° 20.613' W 81° 34.382'
Obliterated by dam

Onaping Falls
Northeastern Region
Type: Cascade Type
River and County: Onaping River, Levack Station, Sudbury County
GPS Location: N 46° 35.307' W 81° 22.965'
Rating: 4/4
Access: Moderate, 10 Minute

Description: This is a great destination and excellent for a family outing. There are multiple trails and lookout points from which to explore and view these falls.

Getting There: Head west on Trans-Canada Hwy/ON-17 for 14.6 km and exit onto NW Bypass/ON-144 N toward Timmins. After 17.8 km., turn left onto ON-144 North and you will arrive at the falls after about 19 km.

Photography Tips: Leave yourself plenty of time as there is much to explore at this falls. You will have no problem in finding great photo setups from multiple positions.

Nearby Attractions: The Larchwood Cascade is nearby although it is not impressive.

Plunge Falls, Northeast Region, Sudbury County, Espanola
Plunge Type, Little Hannah Lake, Rating: 1/4, Access: Moderate
GPS Location: N 46° 12.004' W 81° 32.987'
Canoe

Sagamok Falls, Northeast Region, Sudbury County, La Cloch P.P.
Waterfall Type, La Cloche Creek, Rating: 1/4, Access: Easy
GPS Location: N 46° 06.800' W 82° 04.597'
At the end of Unnamed Rd in La Cloch P.P.

Secord Road Cascade, Northeast Region, Sudbury County,
McFarlane Lake
Cascade Type, Wanapitei River, Rating: 1/4, Access: Easy
GPS Location: N 46° 20.700' W 80° 50.322'
Off Secord Rd. south of McFarlane Lake

Seven Sisters Rapids, Northeast Region, Sudbury County, Massey
Rapids Type, Aux Sables River, Rating: 1/4, Access: Moderate
GPS Location: N 46° 13.530' W 82° 04.386'
Off Imperial St. N

Sturgeon Chutes, Northeast Region, Sudbury County, Alban
Chute Type, Wanapitei River, Rating: 1/4, Access: Moderate
GPS Location: N 46° 04.147' W 80° 49.788'
Canoe

The Chutes

Northeast Region
Type: Cascade Type
River and County: Aux Sables River, Massey, Sudbury County
GPS Location: N 46° 13.416' W 82° 04.560'
Rating: 3/4

Access: Moderate trail difficulty, 5 Minutes

Description: A series of cascades can be viewed and enjoyed on the
trail beside the river.
Getting There: Located in The Chutes P.P.
Photography Tips: Plan on spending time along the river trail where
there are multiple points to set up.

Timmins Chute, Northeast Region, Sudbury County, Coniston
Rapids Type, Wanapitei River, Rating: 1/4, Access: Easy
GPS Location: N 46° 31.290' W 80° 42.540'
At the end of Stinson Hydro Rd. east of Coniston

Upper Goose Falls, Northeast Region, Sudbury County, Sturgeon
River P.P.
Cascade Type, Sturgeon River, Rating: 3/4, Access: Moderate
GPS Location: N 46° 58.188' W 80° 27.444'
Canoe

White Pine Chutes, Northeast Region, Sudbury County, McFarlane
Lake
Cascade Type, Wanapitei River, Rating: 1/4, Access: Moderate
GPS Location: N 46° 22.140' W 80° 48.312'
Off Old Wanup Rd. SE of McFarlane Lake

Whitefish Falls, Northeast Region, Sudbury County, Whitefish Falls
Cascade Type, Whitefish River, Rating: 2/4, Access: Easy
GPS Location: N 46° 06.996' W 81° 43.950'
Off ON-6 in Whitefish Falls

Algoma Region

Agawa Falls, Algoma Region, Lake Superior P.P.
Plunge Type, Agawa River, Rating: 3/4, Access: Difficult
GPS Location: N 47° 22.632' W 84° 32.106'
12 hours round trip hike

Airport Road Falls, Algoma Region, Sault St Marie
Cascade Type, Unknown River, Rating: 1/4, Access: Moderate
GPS Location: N 46° 33' W 84° 28.764'
Off Airport Rd

Aubrey Fall

Algoma Region
Type: Irregular Cascade Type
River and County: Mississagi River, Aubrey Falls, Algoma County
GPS Location: N 46° 54.636' W 83° 12.642'
Rating: 4/4
Access: Moderate, 15 Minute

Description: This is a tremendous widespread falls with trails that allow you to access it from many positions. At first you may be disappointed because the dam above holds back the water but it is released daily. When I was there this was done at 11 o'clock. Do not get caught out on the rocks when this happens as you might well be killed.

Getting There: To reach the falls, take Highway 129 north from Highway 17 in Thessalon, and find the signed entrance to Aubrey Falls 9.8 km. past the intersection of Highway 556. Don't be fooled by the signed road to Aubrey Falls Generating Station just before it.

Photography Tips: There are multiple spots to photograph from and you will want a wide lens. The red lichen covered rocks and deep green pines provide excellent elements.

Nearby Attractions: Grindstone Falls is about 45 minutes away south.

Baldhead River Falls, Algoma Region, Lake Superior P.P.
Cascade Type, Baldhead River, Rating: 2/4, Access: Moderate
GPS Location: N 47° 29.322' W 84° 50.231'
4 hour round trip hike on orphan Lake Trail

Batchawana Falls

Algoma Region

Type: Plunge Type
River and County: Batchawana River, Batchawana Bay, Algoma County
GPS Location: N 46° 59.224' W 84° 31.448'
Rating: 3/4
Access: Moderate to difficult, 20 Minutes

Description: This is a gorgeous waterfall in a wilderness type of
environment
Getting There: Take Batchawana Bay Road north off Highway 17
about 61 km north of Sault St Marie. This is a logging road and may be
unmarked. The falls is by the side of the road after about 8.6 miles. Be
very careful, as this is a logging road. It is narrow and rough in parts
and it could be very dangerous to meet a logging truck from the other
direction.
Photography Tips: There is a pull off area by the falls and it is easy to
take photographs from here. The color and view are spectacular in the
autumn. You may be able to work your way down but don't approach
it if you don't feel very confident. You would be better to go with
someone and to let others know where you are going.
Nearby Attractions: Chippewa Falls is on the road from Sault St Marie.

Beaver Falls, Algoma Region, Island Lake
Cascade Type, Northland Creek, Rating: 2/4, Access: Easy
GPS Location: N 46° 44.356' W 84° 08.015'
Off Highway 556, 19.6 km north of Highway 17

Bellevue Creek Falls, Algoma Region, Northland
Waterfall Type, Bellevue Creek, Rating: 2/4, Access: Moderate
GPS Location: N 46° 42.630' W 84° 13.908'
Off Bellevue Valley Rd. 0.5 km north of ON-556

Bells Falls, Algoma Region, Bellingham
Cascade Type, Little White River, Rating: 2/4, Access: Easy
GPS Location: N 46° 23.602' W 83° 17.232'
Off Algoma Rd 554 by bridge over Little White River

Big Carp River Falls, Algoma Region, Sault St Marie
Cascade Type, Big Carp River, Rating: 1/4, Access: Easy
GPS Location: N 46° 32.022' W 84° 32.718'
500 m. north of Second Line W and east of Marshall Drive

Black Beaver Falls North
Algoma Region
Type: Cascade Type
River and County: Beaver Creek, Agawa Bay, Algoma County
GPS Location: N 47° 25.098' W 84° 29.046'
Rating: 3/4
Access: Moderate Difficulty, 15 Minutes

Description: A beautiful waterfall in a gorgeous setting, especially in the fall when you are most likely to take the Agawa Train tour.
Getting There: The trip to this falls from the train stop can be along the river trail or along the tracks and will take about 15 minutes one way. See the map here.
Photography Tips: There are a couple of aspects from the viewing platform which are excellent. Colorful fall foliage surrounds it, so look for a wide lens to use.
Nearby Attractions: Black Beaver Falls South is only a short distance away and Otter Falls and Bridal Veil Falls are nearby.

Black Beaver Falls South

Algoma Region

Type: Cascade Type
River and County: Beaver Creek, Agawa Bay, Algoma County
GPS Location: N 47° 25.098' W 84° 29.046'
Rating: 3/4
Access: Moderate Difficulty, 15 Minutes

Description: This is a gorgeous falls, especially in the fall when you are most likely to take the Agawa Train tour.
Getting There: The trip to this falls from the train stop can be along the river trail or along the tracks and will take about 15 minutes one way. See the map here.
Photography Tips: There are a couple of aspects from the viewing platform which are excellent. Colorful fall foliage surrounds it, so look for a wide lens to use.
Nearby Attractions: Black Beaver Falls North is only a short distance away and Otter Falls and Bridal Veil Falls are nearby.

Bridal Veil Falls

Algoma Region
Type: Cascade Type
River and County: Agawa River, Agawa Bay, Algoma County

GPS Location: N 47° 25.098' W 84° 29.046'
Rating: 3/4
Access: Easy, 20 Minutes

Description: This is the most impressive of the four Agawa Canyon
waterfalls. It falls in two sections against a gorgeous natural setting.
Getting There: The trip to this falls from the train stop can be along
the river trail or along the tracks and will take about 20 minutes one
way. See the map here.
Photography Tips: Colorful fall foliage surrounds it, so look for a wide
lens to use. Agawa River offers some nice reflections and there are
some interesting side views as you approach the falls.
Nearby Attractions: Black Beaver Falls North and South, and Otter
Falls are nearby.

Cataract Falls, Algoma Region, Bind River
Cascade Type, Bind River, Rating: 1/4, Access: Easy
GPS Location: N 46° 15.426' W 82°58.710'
Off ON-557

Chippewa Falls Lower

Algoma Region
Type: Cascade Type
River and County: Chippewa River, Chippewa Falls, Algoma County
GPS Location: N 46° 55.752' W 84° 25.516'
Rating: 3/4
Access: Easy difficulty, 5 Minute

Description: Easy to reach, Chippewa Falls, both upper and lower, are among Algoma's greatest falls. There is a wealth of excellent views along the trails.
Getting There: From Sault St Marie go northwest on the Trans-Canada Highway/ On-17/ Great Northern Road for 46.8 km and you will see it on the right. There is a parking lot and trails to the falls.
Photography Tips: There is an extended rock ledge which is situated close to the falls which offers excellent set up spots. You can also get longer views from the highway.
Nearby Attractions: Beaver and Batchawana Falls.

Chippewa Falls Upper

Algoma Region
Type: Cascade Type

River and County: Chippewa River, Chippewa Falls, Algoma County
GPS Location: N 46° 55.752' W 84° 25.516'
Rating: 3/4
Access: Moderate difficulty, 20 Minute

Description: Easy to reach, Chippewa Falls, both upper and lower, are among Algoma's greatest falls. There is a wealth of excellent views along the trails.
Getting There: From Sault St Marie go northwest on the Trans-Canada Highway/ On-17/ Great Northern Road for 46.8 km and you will see it on the right. There is a parking lot and trails to the falls.
Photography Tips: The dark green pines offer an excellent background to the reddish rock along the banks of this falls.
Nearby Attractions: Beaver and Batchawana Falls.

Coldwater River Falls, Algoma Region, Lake Superior P.P.
Cascade Type, Coldwater River, Rating: 3/4, Access: Difficult
GPS Location: N 47° 28.152' W 84° 45.816'
Canoe or extended hike

Crystal Falls

Algoma Region
Type: Cascade Type
River and County: Crystal Creek, Sault St Marie, Algoma County
GPS Location: N 46° 35.386' W 84° 16.551'
Rating: 3/4
Access: Easy Trail difficulty, 5 Minutes

Description: A wonderful steep cascade found right in the town of Sault St Marie. Great spot for a family outing and picnic.
Getting There: From the Great Northern Road/Trans- Canada Highway go east on 5th Line, continuing on Landslide Road and you will find the Kinsmen Park. Drive to the end of the road to a parking area. Take the trail to the right, and you will find various boardwalks and structures about the falls.
Photography Tips: The stairs along the side of this steep falls give multiple points of view.
Nearby Attractions: Minnehaha Falls is in the same park.

Dore Falls, Algoma Region, Michipicoten Harbour
Dore River, Rating: 1/4, Access: Private
GPS Location: N 47° 58.345' W 84° 56.225'
Private, permission needed

Goulais River Falls, Algoma Region, Goulais River P.P.
Cascade Type, Goulais River, Rating: 2/4, Access: Moderate
GPS Location: N 46° 54.155' W 83° 57.485'
Unnamed road in Goulais River P.P.

Granary Creek Falls, Algoma Region, Blind River
Granary Creek River, Rating: 2/4, Access: Moderate
GPS Location: N 46° 14.185' W 82° 54.195'
Found off Granary Lake Road 8 km north of Blind River

Grand Falls, Algoma Region, Cummings Lake
Irregular cascade Type, Cummings Lake, Rating: 1/4, Access: Easy
GPS Location: N 46° 27.283' W 83° 21.667'
Off ON-129 in Cummings Lake

Grindstone Falls, Algoma Region, Grindstone Creek
Slide Type, Grindstone Creek, Rating: 2/4, Access: Easy
GPS Location: N 46° 41.466' W 83° 22.440'
Off ON-129, look for small sign 3 km. north of Lafoe Cr. sign

Harmony River Falls, Algoma Region, Harmony Beach
Cascade Type, Harmony River, Rating: 1/4, Access: Easy
GPS Location: N 46° 50.934' W 84° 20.988'
0.1 km east on unnamed rd from Harmony Beach

High Falls (Blind River), Algoma Region, Blind River
Plunge Type, Blind River, Rating: 2/4, Access: Difficult
GPS Location: N 46° 18.036' W 83° 03.900'
Canoe or extended hike

Kennebec Falls, Algoma Region, Massey
Cascade Type, Serpent River, Rating: 1/4, Access: Easy
GPS Location: N 46° 12.702' W 82° 30.666'
33 km east of Massey off the Trans-Canada Highway

Lady Evelyn Falls, Algoma Region, Lake Superior P.P.
Cascade Type, Sand River, Rating: 4/4, Access: Difficult
GPS Location: N 47° 28.535' W 84° 39.095'
Canoe

Little Rapids, Algoma Region, Little Rapids
Irregular cascade Type, Little Thessalon River, Rating: 2/4, Access:
Easy
GPS Location: N 46° 18.215' W 83° 33.065'
Off Little Rapids Rd south of Ansonia Rd.

McPhail Falls, Algoma Region, Wawa
Dam, Michipicoten River, Rating: 1/4, Access: None
GPS Location: N 47° 58.485' W 84° 48.005'
Obliterated by Dam

Michipicoton Harbour Rd Falls, Algoma Region, Michipicoton
Plunge Type, Michipicoton River, Rating: 2/4, Access: Moderate
GPS Location: N 47° 57.717' W 84° 53.417'
Off Michipicoton River Village Rd., 7 km south of ON-17

Minnehaha Falls, Algoma Region, Sault St Marie
Irregular Cascade Type, Crystal Creek, Rating: 2/4, Access: Easy
GPS Location: N 46° 35.386' W 84° 16.551'
At Kinsmen Park on 5th Line

Mississagi Falls, Algoma Region, Blind River
Irregular Cascade Type, Mississagi River, Rating: 1/4, Access: Easy
GPS Location: N 46° 12.030' W 83° 01.662'
Found just west of the ON-17, 5 km west of Blind River

Montreal River Chasm, Algoma Region, Agawa Bay
Plunge Type, Montreal River, Rating: 1/4, Access: Easy
GPS Location: N 47° 14.298' W 84° 38.669'
By ON-17 just south of lake Superior P.P., often dry

Otter Falls, Algoma Region, Agawa Bay
Cascade Type, Otter Creek, Rating: 2/4, Access: Easy
GPS Location: N 47° 25.098' W 84° 29.046'
Found on the Agawa Canyon Train Trip

Pancake Falls, Algoma Region, Pancake Bay P.P.
Cascade Type, Pancake River, Rating: 2/4, Access: Moderate
GPS Location: N 46° 58.165' W 84° 42.115'
8 km. round trip hike in Pancake Bay P.P.

Pecors Falls, Algoma Region, Elliot Lake
Dam, River, Rating: 1/4, Access: Difficult
GPS Location: N 46° 23.250' W 82° 25.302'
Canoe, compromised by dam

Potholes Falls, Algoma Region, Potholes P.P.
Plunge Type, Kiniwabi River, Rating: 3/4, Access: Moderate
GPS Location: N 47° 57.246' W 84° 16.146'
At Potholes P.P. 52.3 miles west of Wawa

Robertson Creek Falls, Algoma Region, Bourdages Corners
Cascade Type, Robertson Creek, Rating: 3/4, Access: Difficult
GPS Location: N 46° 46.065' W 84° 17.375'
At end of Robinson Lake Road down a steep bank

Root Falls, Algoma Region, Odena
Root River, Rating: 2/4, Access: Moderate
GPS Location: N 46° 35.495' W 84° 17.345'
By 6th Line East just east of ON-17

Sand River Falls Lower

Type: Cascade Type
River and County: Sand River, Lake Superior P.P., Algoma County
GPS Location: N 47° 25.972' W 84° 43.867'
Rating: 3/4
Access: Easy trail difficulty, 5 Minutes

Description: Take the Pinguisibi Trail, and a couple of minutes will
bring you to the Lower Falls. This natural setting seems to be a favorite
of fishermen as well. There is a lot to explore before moving on to the
Upper Falls.
Getting There: This falls is found in Lake Superior Provincial Falls by
the Trans-Canada Highway about 71 km south of Wawa. The lot has a
fee ($5.25 in 2010) and you need to have coins.
Photography Tips: There are numerous place to move onto the rock
ledges with excellent backgrounds, especially in fall.
Nearby Attractions: Sand River Upper Falls

Sand River Falls Upper
Algoma Region
Type: Cascade Type

River and County: Sand River, Lake Superior P.P., Algoma County
GPS Location: N 47° 25.972' W 84° 43.867'
Rating: 3/4
Access: Moderate trail difficulty, 15 Minutes

Description: Take the Pinguisibi Trail, and after visiting the Lower
Falls, a moderate walk of another 10 minutes brings you to the Upper
Falls.
Getting There: This falls is found in Lake Superior Provincial Falls by
the Trans-Canada Highway about 71 km south of Wawa. The lot has a
fee ($5.25 in 2010) and you need to have coins.
Photography Tips: There are numerous place to move onto the rock
ledges with excellent backgrounds, especially in fall.
Nearby Attractions: Sand River Lower Falls

Scott Falls, Algoma Region, Wawa
Dam, Michipicoten River, Rating: 1/4, Access: Easy
GPS Location: N 47° 54.395' W 84° 44.365'
Obliterated by dam

Silver Falls Lower
Algoma Region

Type: Plunge Type
River and County: Magpie River, Wawa, Algoma County
GPS Location: N 47° 56.483' W 84° 49.485'

Rating: 3/4
Access: Easy trail difficulty, 5 Minutes

Description: This falls can have different water levels depending on the amount released upstream but it is always very picturesque.

Getting There: Turn east off the Trans-Canada Highway 5.0 km south of Wawa on High Falls Rd and after 0.1 km turn right on Queen St and then left on Blue Ave/ Michipicoten Rd where you will find the falls in a short distance. The trail on the east side brings you to the falls after first passing.

Photography Tips: Near the bottom there is an excellent shot with a pool of water in the foreground. There are also excellent shots near the crest.

Nearby Attractions: Silver Falls Upper, Wawa Falls

Silver Falls Upper
Algoma Region
Type: Plunge Type
River and County: Magpie River, Wawa, Algoma County

GPS Location: N 47° 56.483' W 84° 49.485'
Rating: 3/4
Access: Easy trail difficulty, 10 Minutes

Description: This falls can have different water levels depending on the amount released upstream but it is always worth visiting.
Getting There: Turn east off the Trans-Canada Highway 5.0 km south of Wawa on High Falls Rd and after 0.1 km turn right on Queen St and then left on Blue Ave/ Michipicoten Rd where you will find the falls in a short distance. The trail on the east side brings you to the falls after first passing the lower falls.
Photography Tips: There is a nice long shot just past the crest of the lower falls.
Nearby Attractions: Silver Falls Lower, Wawa Falls

Speckled Trout Falls, Algoma Region, Lake Superior P.P.
Cascade Type, River, Rating: 2/4, Access: Difficult
GPS Location: N 47° 18.516' W 84° 36.094'
Extended hike
Split Rock Rapids, Algoma Region, Missiniabi P.P.
Rapids Type, Missiniabi River, Rating: 2/4, Access: Difficult
GPS Location: N 48° 46.425' W 83° 26.595'
Canoe, in Missiniabi P.P.
Steep Hill Falls, Algoma Region, Wawa
Dam, Magpie River, Rating: 1/4, Access: Easy
GPS Location: N 48° 04.816'W 84° 44.583'
Obliterated by dam

Thessalon Falls Lower, Algoma Region, Thessalon
Cascade Type, Thessalon River, Rating: 2/4, Access: Easy
GPS Location: N 46° 37.515' W 83° 33.155'
4 km from Carpenter Lake Cabins

Thessalon Falls Upper, Algoma Region, Thessalon
Cascade Type, Thessalon River, Rating: 2/4, Access: Easy
GPS Location: N 46° 37.475' W 83° 33.175'
6 km from Carpenter Lake Cabins

Thunder Falls, Algoma Region, Missiniabi P.P.
Missiniabi River, Rating: 3/4, Access: Difficult
GPS Location: N 48° 49.365' W 83° 21.445'
Canoe or extended hike

Wawa Falls (Magpie Falls)
Algoma Region
Type: Cascade Type
River and County: Magpie River, Wawa, Algoma County
GPS Location: N 47° 57.542' W 84° 49.670'
Rating: 4/4
Access: Easy trail difficulty, 1 Minutes

Description: This is a wonderful waterfall which has a large crest which
spreads to a huge base. There is a convenient boardwalk from the base
to the crest.

Getting There: From the south end of Wawa go east on Pinewood Dr off the Trans-Canada Highway and follow the signs to the falls. Photography Tips: There are excellent areas to setup at the bottom as well as the top.

Nearby Attractions: Silver Falls

Whitefish Falls (Little Missiniabi River), Algoma Region, Missiniabi Lake
Cascade Type, Little Missiniabi River, Rating: 2/4, Access: Easy
GPS Location: N 48° 21.225 W 83° 40.265
Canoe

Lakehead Region

Kenora County

Nestor Falls, Lakehead Region, Kenora County, Nestor Falls
Cascade Type, Kakabikitchiwan Lake, Rating: 2/4, Access: Easy
GPS Location: N 49° 06.911' W 93° 55.567'
Off ON-71 in Nestor Falls

Oak Falls, Lakehead Region, Kenora County, West English River P.P.
Cascade Type, West English River, Rating: 3/4, Access: Moderate
GPS Location: N 50° 27.576' W 93° 48.996'
Canoe

Rainy River County

Canyon Falls, Lakehead Region, Rainy River County, Quetico P.P.
Cascade Type, Atikokan River, Rating: 2/4, Access: Difficult
GPS Location: N 48° 19.074' W 91° 07.362'
Canoe

Little Falls, Lakehead Region, Rainy River County, Quetico P.P.
Cascade Type, Atikokan River, Rating: 2/4, Access: Difficult
GPS Location: N 48° 18.906' W 91° 06.720'
Canoe

Kennebas Falls, Lakehead Region, Rainy River County, Quetico P.P.
Cascade Type, Atikokan River, Rating: 2/4, Access: Difficult
GPS Location: N 48° 19.572' W 91° 08.046
Canoe

Koko Falls, Lakehead Region, Rainy River County, Quetico P.P.
Cascade Type, Atikokan River, Rating: 2/4, Access: Difficult
GPS Location: N 48° 18.966' W 91° 06.948'
Canoe

Silver Falls (Atikokan River), Lakehead Region, Rainy River County, Douglas Island
Cascade Type, Atikokan River, Rating: 2/4, Access: Difficult
GPS Location: N 48° 13.914' W 91° 03.367'
Canoe

Snake Falls, Lakehead Region, Rainy River County, Douglas Island
Cascade Type, Atikokan River, Rating: 2/4, Access: Difficult
GPS Location: N 48° 23.316' W 92° 10.332'
Canoe

Split Rock Falls, Lakehead Region, Rainy River County, Quetico P.P.
Cascade Type, Atikokan River, Rating: 2/4, Access: Difficult
GPS Location: N 48° 27.258' W 91° 24.258'
Canoe

Thunder Bay County

Aguasabon Falls, Lakehead Region, Thunder Bay County

Type: Plunge
River and County: Aguasabon River, Terrace Bay, Thunder Bay County

GPS Location: N 48° 46.728' W 87° 07.254'

Rating: 4/4
Access: Easy trail difficulty, 2 Minutes

Description: This is a tremendous falls, especially when there is a lot of water flowing through.
The falls plunges and follows a steep narrow gorge.

Getting There: At the east end of Terrace Bay, take Aguasabon Gorge Rd. and drive to the end. At the parking lot there is a trail and boardwalk to an overlook of the falls.

Photography Tips: The viewing platform is perhaps the most impressive view.

Nearby Attractions: Rainbow Falls is a short Drive

Alexander Falls, Lakehead Region, Thunder Bay County, Cameron Falls
Dam, Nipigon River, Rating: 1/4, Access: Easy
GPS Location: N 49° 08.080' W 88° 21.588'
Obliterated by dam

Angler Falls, Lakehead Region, Thunder Bay County, White River
Cascade Type, White River, Rating: 3/4, Access: Moderate
GPS Location: N 48° 34.984' W 85° 53.538'
Canoe or hike

Cameron Falls (Nipigon River), Lakehead Region, Thunder Bay County, Cameron Falls
Dam, Nipigon River, Rating: 1/4, Access: Easy
GPS Location: N 49° 09.198' W 88° 20.742'
Obliterated by dam

Cascade Falls (Cascade River), Lakehead Region, Thunder Bay County, Pukaskwa N. P.
Cascade Type, Cascade River, Rating: 2/4, Access: Difficult
GPS Location: N 48° 07.998' W 86° 02.832'
Canoe

Cascade Falls (Current River), Lakehead Region, Thunder Bay County, Cascades Conservation Area
Cascade Type, Current River, Rating: 2/4, Access: Moderate
GPS Location: N 48° 30.006' W 89° 13.458'
From trail in Cascades Conservation Area

Chigamiwinigun Falls, Lakehead Region, Thunder Bay County, Pukaskwa P.P.
Cascade Type, White River, Rating: 4/4, Access: Moderate
GPS Location: N 48° 33.510' W 86° 13.926'
Canoe

Dead Horse Creek Falls, Lakehead Region, Thunder Bay County, Marathon
Cascade Type, Dead Horse Creek, Rating: 2/4, Access: Moderate
GPS Location: N 48° 48.888' W 86° 41.118'
Off ON-17 west of Marathon

Denison Falls, Lakehead Region, Thunder Bay County, Nimoosh P.P.
Cascade Type, Dog River, Rating: 4/4, Access: Moderate
GPS Location: N 47° 58.415' W 85° 12.175'
Canoe

Dog Falls, Lakehead Region, Thunder Bay County, Silver Falls P.P.
Cascade Type, Kaministiquia River, Rating: 4/4, Access: Difficult
GPS Location: N 48° 40.056' W 89° 36.300'
Canoe

High Falls (Kaministiquia River), Lakehead Region, Thunder Bay County, Silver Falls P.P.
Cascade Type, Kaministiquia River, Rating: 2/4, Access: Difficult
GPS Location: N 48° 41.406' W 89° 38.412'
Canoe

High Falls of the Pigeon River, Lakehead Region

Type: Plunge Type
River and County: Pigeon River, Pigeon River PP, Thunder Bay County
GPS Location: N 48° 00.288' W 89° 35.874'

Rating: 4/4
Access: Moderate trail difficulty, 15 Minutes

Description:
This falls is located on the border of the State of Minnesota and the Province of Ontario and is spectacular in all season.

Getting There:
You can take the trail to the falls from Pigeon River PP but it is a fair hike particularly in winter. An easier route is to cross into Minnesota and immediately turn into Grande Portage State Park

Photography Tips:
It is easy to work this falls from various distances to take full advantage of it.
Nearby Attractions:
Middle Falls of Pigeon River and Partridge Falls are nearby

Hume Falls, Lakehead Region, Thunder Bay County, Kakabeka Falls Cascade Type, Kaministiquia River, Rating: 2/4, Access: Moderate
GPS Location: N 48° 26.160' W 89° 34.938'
Off the end of Hume Rd in Kakabeka Falls

Kakabeka Falls, Lakehead Region

Type: Cascade Type
River and County: Kaministiquia River, Kakabeka Falls, Thunder Bay
County
GPS Location: N 48° 24.177' W 89° 37.457'

Rating: 4/4
Access: Easy trail difficulty, 2 Minutes

Description: One of Ontario's most spectacular falls, it is also easy to
get to and to view from many angles.

Getting There: From Thunder Bay go west on Highway 11 for about
25 km. and at the west end of the Town of Kakabeka Falls, you will see
Kakabeka Falls Provincial Park. After parking in the lot you will need
tp pay the day use fee.

Photography Tips: There are boardwalks and observation points on
both sides of the river to provide a wide variety of set up points. You
might also want to use a longer lens to catch details.

Nearby Attractions: Hume Falls is nearby.

Kinghorn Falls, Lakehead Region, Thunder Bay County, Jellicoe
Cascade Type, Namewaminikan River, Rating: 1/4, Access: Moderate
GPS Location: N 49° 43.410' W 87° 26.868'
Off Unnamed Rd north of ON-11 east of Jellicoe

Last Falls Cypress, Lakehead Region, Thunder Bay County, Town
Waterfall Type, Cypress River, Rating: 3/4, Access: Difficult
GPS Location: N 48° 57.286' W 87° 50.994
Canoe

Lenore Lakes Falls, Lakehead Region, Thunder Bay County, Lenore
Cascade Type, Lenore Lake, Rating: 1/4, Access: Easy
GPS Location: N 48° 28.200' W 89° 34.560'
End of Lake Lenore Rd off ON-61

Long Rapids, Lakehead Region, Thunder Bay County, Beardmore
Rapids Type, Sturgeon River, Rating: 2/4, Access: Moderate
GPS Location: N 49° 43.044' W 87° 59.178'
Off Camp 72 Rd north of Beardmore

MacKenzie Falls, Lakehead Region, Thunder Bay County, Current River
Cascade Type, MacKenzie River, Rating: 2/4, Access: Moderate
GPS Location: N 48° 32.598' W 88° 56.244'
Off McKenzie Heights Rd. east of Current River

Mazukama Creek Falls, Lakehead Region, Thunder Bay County, Nipigon
Cascade Type, Mazukama Creek, Rating: 3/4, Access: Moderate
GPS Location: N 49° 00.732' W 88° 00.204'
Off ON-17 east of Nipigon

Middle Falls of the Pigeon River, Lakehead Region, Thunder Bay County, Pigeon River P.P.
Waterfall Type, Pigeon River, Rating: 2/4, Access: Moderate
GPS Location: N 48° 00.761' W 89° 36.966'
Off ON-593 in Pigeon River P.P.

Middle Falls Cypress, Lakehead Region, Thunder Bay County, Town
Waterfall Type, Cypress River, Rating: 3/4, Access: Difficult
GPS Location: N 48° 58.118' W 87.° 49.889'
Canoe

Mink Creek Falls, Lakehead Region, Thunder Bay County, Marathon
Cascade Type, Mink Creek, Rating: 3/4, Access: Moderate
GPS Location: N 48° 46.116' W 86° 30.702'
Off ON-17 west of Marathon

Partridge Falls, Lakehead Region, Thunder Bay County, La
Verendrye P.P.
Waterfall Type, Pigeon River, Rating: 3/4, Access: Easy
GPS Location: N 47° 59.694' W 89° 50.724'
Off Partridge Falls Rd (Minnesota) It is closed in winter

Pine River Falls, Lakehead Region, Thunder Bay County, Crooks
Cascade Type, Pine River, Rating: 3/4, Access: Easy
GPS Location: N 48° 44.034' W 89° 33.851'
Off Unnamed Rd west of ON-61 and Crooks

Port Arthur Spillway, Lakehead Region, Thunder Bay County,
Thunder Bay
Slide Type, River, Rating: 2/4, Access: Easy
GPS Location: N 48° 27.264' W 89° 11.316'
Off Cumberland St. in Thunder Bay

Rainbow Falls, Lakehead Region, Thunder Bay County, Rainbow
Falls P.P.
Cascade Type, Hewitson River, Rating: 4/4, Access: Moderate
GPS Location: N 48° 50.802' W 87° 23.982'
In Rainbow Falls P.P. 2 km. trail from Visitors Center

Schist Falls, Lakehead Region, Thunder Bay County, Pukaskwa N.P.
Cascade Type, Pukaskwa River, Rating: 3/4, Access: Difficult
GPS Location: N 48° 00.366' W 85° 53.148'
Canoe

Sevignys Creek Falls, Lakehead Region, County, Thunder Bay
Cascade Type, Sevignys Creek, Rating: 2/4, Access: Easy
GPS Location: N 48° 29.160' W 89° 11.070'
Off Copenhagen Rd in Thunder Bay

Silver Falls (Kaministiquia River), Lakehead Region, Thunder Bay
County, Silver Falls P.P.
Cascade Type, Kaministiquia River, Rating: 3/4, Access: Difficult
GPS Location: N 48° 39.588' W 89° 35.910'
Canoe

Split Falls, Lakehead Region, Thunder Bay County, Kakabeka Falls
Cascade Type, Kaministiquia River, Rating: 1/4, Access: Moderate
GPS Location: N 48° 26.898' W 89° 34.713'
Off Torrie Rd NE of Kakabeka Falls

Spring Falls, Lakehead Region, Thunder Bay County, Nipigon
Cascade Type, River, Rating: 2/4, Access: Easy
GPS Location: N 49° 19.986' W 88° 17.302'
Off ON-11 north of Nipigon

Trowbridge Falls, Lakehead Region, Thunder Bay County, Thunder
Bay
Cascade Type, Current River, Rating: 2/4, Access: Easy
GPS Location: N 48° 29.406' W 89° 11.358'
Off Trowbridge Rd in Thunder Bay

Twin Falls, Lakehead Region, Thunder Bay County, Manitouwadge
Cascade Type, Kagiano River , Rating: 3/4, Access: Difficult
GPS Location: N 49° 11.184' W 86° 07.032'
Off rough Unnamed Rd west of Manitouwadge

Umbata Falls, Lakehead Region, Thunder Bay County, White River
Cascade Type, White River, Rating: 4/4, Access: Moderate
GPS Location: N 48° 32.250' W 86° 08.376'
Off Unnamed Rd south of ON-17

Upper Falls on Cypress, Lakehead Region, Thunder Bay County, Town
Waterfall Type, Cypress River, Rating: 3/4, Access: Difficult
GPS Location: N 87° 47.892 W 48° 59.989'
Canoe

Other Resources

Websites
Nature Notes by Harold Stiver
http://www.ontfin.com/Word/ontario-waterfalls/

Waterfalls of Ontario by Mark Harris
http://waterfallsofontario.com/

Great Lakes Waterfalls
http://gowaterfalling.com/

Hamilton Waterfalls
http://www.waterfalls.hamilton.ca/

Hamilton- City of Waterfalls
http://www.cityofwaterfalls.ca/

Ontario Waterfalls Facebook Page
https://www.facebook.com/Ontario.Waterfalls

Hamilton Waterfalls Facebook Page
https://www.facebook.com/groups/13358248908/

Ontario Waterfalls Twitter
https://twitter.com/OntWaterfalls

Other Books by Harold Stiver

Unless noted, there are Print and eBook editions available for the following. They are available at many places including Amazon, Barnes & Noble and Kobo

Birding Guide to Orkney

Ontario's Old Mills

Connecticut Covered Bridges (eBook)
Indiana Covered Bridges
Maine Covered Bridges (eBook)
Massachusetts Covered Bridges (eBook)
Michigan Covered Bridges (eBook)
New England Covered Bridges
New Hampshire Covered Bridges
New York Covered Bridges
The Covered Bridges of Kentucky (eBook)
The Covered Bridges of Kentucky and Tennessee
The Covered Bridges of Tennessee (eBook)
Vermont's Covered Bridges
The Covered Bridges of Virginia (eBook)
The Covered Bridges of Virginia and West Virginia
The Covered Bridges of West Virginia (eBook)

Index

A

B

Broadbent Falls	138	Broman Falls	45
Brooks Falls	138	Brown Falls	45
Bullhead Falls	91	Bunny Trail Falls	139
Burk's Falls	139	Burleigh Falls	120
Buttermilk Falls Hamilton	45	Buttermilk (Forest Mills)	114
Buttermilk (Haliburton)	82		

C

Callaghan Rapids	107	Cameron Falls	148
Cameron Falls (Nipigon)	175	Campbellford Rapids	116
Canning Falls Lower	69	Canning Falls Upper	69
Canterbury Falls	45	Canyon Falls	173
Carcajou Falls	130	Cardinal Creek	117
Carleton Place Cascade	112	Cascade Falls	148
Cascade Falls (Cascade)	175	Cascade (Current R.)	176
Cascade Rapids	130	Castor Oil Chute	82
Cataract Falls	161	Cave Falls	45
Cedar Lake Falls	130	Centennial Falls	45
Centre Falls	149	Chaffey Lock Cascade	112
Chapmans Chute	139	Chartrand Corners	149
Chat Falls	117	Chaudiere Falls	117
Chedoke Falls	47	Chedoke Lower	46
Chigamiwinigun Falls	176	Chippewa Falls	161
Chippewa Falls Upper	162	Chisholm Mills	108
Churches Falls	78	Churches Upper	78
Clappison Falls	48	Clark Falls	91
Cliffview Falls	48	Cliffview Lower	48
Cody Rapids	139	Coldwater River	163
Colpoys Falls	69	Conniston Hydro Dam	149
Conroy Rapids	127	Coopers Falls	105
Cope Falls	82	Cordova Falls	108
Corkery Falls	139	Cox Chute	139
Crooked Chute	130	Crooked Rap (French)	140
Crooked Slide	114	Crow River Falls	131
Crowe Bridge Rapids	116	Crozier Falls	91
Crystal Falls (Algoma)	163	Crystal (Sturgeon)	131
Curtain Chute	91	Cypress Lake Outlet	69

WXYZ

Wall Falls	66	Walnut Grove Falls	66
Walters Falls	75	Warsaw Caves Falls	122
Wasdell Rapids	105	Washboard Falls	66
Wasi Cascade	148	Wasi Falls	148
Waterdown Falls	53	Wawa Falls	171
Wawaitan Falls	128	Weaver Creek Falls	75
Webster's Falls	67	Weir's Falls	68
West 18 Mile	41	West Iroquoia Falls	68
West McNeilly Falls	68	West of Fifty Cascade	68
West of Fifty Lower Falls 64		West of Fifty Lower Falls 64	
West of Fifty Upper Cascade 68		Westcliffe Falls	68
Westcliffe Falls Lower 68		White Horse Rapids	137
White Pine Chutes	155	Whitefish Falls	155
Whitefish Falls (Little Missiniabi River)		172	
Whitefish Rapids	107	Whites Falls	103
Wilsons Falls	103	Winona Falls	68
Witney Rapids	88	Yarker Falls	115

Made in the USA
Middletown, DE
21 August 2021

46595377R00110